Dedicated to those who arrived
in Austria as young children.
And for those who overcame
the daunting challenges.
And to those who succumbed
and were swooped down like bats
In whichever way you have left
foot tracks that cannot be washed away.

Cover design and Book layout by
Omni Druckproduktion & Design, Vienna, Austria, omnidruck.at

ESTHER WAITHERA KIEBERGER

Challenges of African diaspora in Austria

Content

Chapter 1

Unusual job

'Breathe in deeply! Open the window! Put head your out!
That is good, go out and get some rest and fresh air', said the head cleaner Werner.
Keisha spoke like a two year old. 'My stomach is bad, and I feel nausea'. She held her mouth tight. Then she heard a long clang of the door. The woman who had a black hoodie held her hand and led her down the stairs, and out in the backyard where they had packed the van with their cleaning utensil. She asked Keisha to rest in the front seat, and to drink the cold water she held out for her.
'You will soon feel better!
'Is this your first time?
Keisha just nodded. She was afraid to open her mouth in case she vomited.
'If this was the kind of job she was expected to do, how would she survive? She wandered. Then she took a sip of the cold water. It brought some short relief.
'I have to earn my daily bread, it is a fight to pay my bills, and worse still my children are waiting for school fees'. She wiped her mouth, and cleaned the sweat that had formed on her forehead.

After a few minutes she gathered courage. She took in a deep breathe of air and then walked up the stairs. At the stairs the woman with a black hoodie gave her a perfume and asked her to smear it on her nose, it would help her not to smell the strong indescribable stench coming from the whole house. She was not sure what the smell was but indeed it was strong but she mastered her bravery and followed Danesha, another African woman who was from Gabon, Keisha herself was from Uganda.

Danesha explained to Keisha, 'you know this is unusual job, but we are here to work not to judge what we see or find out why there is a lot of disorder or disorganization in the house; our job is to clean the mess and to put the house in order'. Keisha nodded and took her cleaning trolley that had all the detergents they needed. She had found this job through a Ghanaian man who worked for a church organization that helped people with hoarding disorders, a behavioural pattern manifested by excessive acquisition of things but also an un-willingness to part or throw them away. The result is that the house was full and because of lack of space, the owners had not been able to clean. Dust had settled everywhere, and cobwebs were all over the corners and ceilings.

When Keisha landed in Austria she needed a job, so while attending mass in the African Catholic Community Church, she enquired from the members where she could find a job, and the advise she got was to visit the Africa Sunshine Den, an African restaurant frequented by the majority of the African diaspora in Austria. It was a place where people exchanged information about jobs, legal affairs, News in the country of residence, and from Africa, and they also came mainly to enjoy food and music in the African way. It was here in the Africa Sunshine Den that she met Akan Jackson from Ghana, and he was happy to inform her of an opportunity to work for the church to support a needy group of people.

What Keisha witnessed was that the living room was covered by large amounts of bottles of empty beer, the kitchen too was full, the bedroom was full and only a small part of the bed was free, the bathroom was full and there was no space to bath, and the toilet had no space. It was a very big house with a balcony; that too was full of bottles that were full of urine. Maybe this could explain the stench. As Keisha made thoughts on the kind of person who lived in the place, the others were busy clearing the bottles and collecting all the rubbish that had filled the house. Soon they were making several trips to the big truck that stood at the front door. They moved from one room to the other. Very few words were spoken as they worked like bees. The men carried the heavy bags of rubbish while the head cleaner Werner assessed the quality of things, and sorted them out according to what he thought could be maintained while the dirtiest ones were removed.

That day Keisha was allocated to clean the kitchen. The woman with the black hoodie had spared her from cleaning the toilet and the balcony that was full of dirty bottles. Keisha realized that this kind of disorder could cause health risks, and even have adverse effects on the family and friends. The many bottles brought in had taken over all the space, so that it was impossible to cook in the kitchen or even to have a shower. There was poor sanitation. So many cockroaches could be seen running from one corner to the other.
But it was the big spider that sent Keisha and Danesha running for their lives.
It was Werner who hurried up to find out why the two were screaming.
At first he thought the men in the other room had attacked them.
'Hey! What is it?

Keisha was shaking like a leaf.

'Look at the corner! Up on the ceiling see the big spider!

Werner was irritated. 'You people come from Africa where there are dangerous animals'.

Then he picked up a broom and reached the spider, as he turned around Keisha was already flying down the stairs. This time it was not the stench but a small spider. Suddenly, a moment of relief set in as the men in the other room laughed their heads off. From that day they named Keisha, 'the flying spider'.

The group spent the whole day cleaning up the mess. When they left in the evening the house was clean and fresh. The owner would be happy if not angry that his 'riches of bottles' had been thrown away probably things that he did not want to part with. That day Keisha was exhausted but happy to have survived. She went to bed early and waited for the next assignment.

When her phone rang at six in the morning she received instructions to meet the driver of their van near the church. Keisha quietly hurried and arrived as instructed. This time they were driving out of town to a village near Mödling. The owner was not at home but Werner opened the door. This time the person had collected advertising magazine, newspapers and shopping bags. Keisha wandered.

'Were these things really useful?

'Why did the person keep them? I mean these are useless things. The shopping bags are dirty! The house was inaccessible. The door could not open widely!

'How did he get in?'

All these questions puzzled Keisha.

Werner asked them to wait as he went to the back door to find a way into the house.

He managed to open a window and climbed in.

Then he walked on the papers and decided how best to create space so that the door could open widely otherwise the bigger items would not be removed. Werner opened the window and asked his troop to wait as he passed the rubbish to them. As soon as he had created room near the window the next man got in, and slowly they advanced towards the door. Once the door was free the rest moved in and began filling up bags with papers, which had overtaken all the space in he house. It was impossible to make a picture of how this person operated.

'The dining table was full

The coach and chairs were full

So where did he sit?

The bed was full so where did he sleep?

The curtains were drawn and no light or fresh air reached the house. The only difference this time was that the stench in this house was manageable, thought Keisha.

This opinion would soon change when Werner took them to the first district in Vienna, a tourist attraction, a place full of people, and expensive things.

The penthouse was big. Only a very rich person could afford it or someone who had inherited a fortune, thought Keisha. As Keisha and her co-workers arrived at the house nothing betrayed anything unusual. The outside illuminated class and money and wellbeing. The white marble and gold linings on the corridor just increased their curiosity. It was a beautiful place till the door opened.

This time everyone held their nose. Even Werner the bravest

of all put on a mask and asked everyone else to do so. The details of what they saw have been left out in this narrative; it is left to the imagination of the reader. But it is important to mention that the house had been turned into a toilet. There was no place to step on.

Werner asked his entire troop to step out. He prepared them psychologically on how to approach the cleaning task. This time he asked them to dress in proper protection clothing, to wear long gloves and safety boots. Then they entered the house and cleaned it thoroughly, before they left they installed an equipment to kill all germs and to freshen up the air.

Keisha tried to search her head for this kind of illness.

Then she remembered that in her own country there were people who used to collect trash and fill up their homes. In her mind she could see the village madwoman collecting every single paper on the road. A lot of people did not have any understanding for her and instead chased her away. Sometimes this woman was beaten but what Keisha did not understand was how she managed to get pregnant and bear children yet they termed her a mad woman. Keisha realized that it was a disorder that could be dealt with.

The next experience was in a house not far from her apartment.

What shocked her is that the house was full of unopened items. New items bought in shops and supermarkets. Clothing still in their original packets, perfumes, nail polish, face creams, and dozens of food stuff tins that had expired but still filled the cellar. These items had left no space in all the rooms. The sinks and bathtubs were full only a small sitting corner had survived the invasion of goods. As Werner

entered the house, he found the woman who had refused to leave the house. She wanted to supervise her
'wealth', and to decide what could be discarded; but it was not so easy as the entire troop thought.

Whenever an item was on its way out she raised alarm and caused too many arguments that Werner decided to call off the cleaning session. He needed to call in a social worker or psychologist to assist them to convince the woman of the dangers of living with hazardous and expired food products. Her home was cluttered to the point that she had no space to lead a normal life.

Keisha's job revealed that the collection of things applied even to huge items like sofas and beds that were piled on top of each other. This was the most difficult work for Keisha because it meant carrying these heavy items out into trucks. Whenever they had such work, Keisha would drop dead in bed, and sometimes slept in her shoes. She was too tired to undress. Every contract they got was unique in its own way. And the level of hoarding differed and the items too differed.

It was after two years that Keisha began to like her work. Without these hoarding cases, she would be without a job, and soon she began to appreciate the complexity of her job, and looked forward to whatever came her way. After all, it was a job like any other, only unusual.

As she joined Danesha in Africa Sunshine Den for their Sunday lunch she explained to her what she had heard from her girlfriend.
'You see Maria from Togo works in homecare with people who are overweight and their life is endangered'. She stop-

ped talking and ordered for her food. 'It is a big challenge to convince people who are addicted to food to stop eating. She says a lot of people eat because of emotional difficulties'.

Danesha looked at her in amazement. 'Yes what about it? Eating food is a problem while people in Africa are dying of hunger? Mmh…

Keisha quickly replied. 'They cry for food, and become aggressive when they do not get fed. It is a disorder but many health systems have not recognised it as a disease. She mentioned that sugar, and fat in big masses is the biggest risk. But because these people cannot control their craving they end up with so many kilos, some up to 340 kgs. For example she mentioned about a young man whose internal organs are being suffocated with big pollsters of fat. Her greatest challenge is to have the young man change his diet. She said that the doctors prescribed a diet with 1,200 calories and with no carbohydrates'. And then she began to eat her food that had just been served.

Immediately, Danesha stopped eating and replied. 'This is new! Food being a problem when I am trying to put some flesh on my buttocks to look like an African woman'.

As they ate their food Keisha continued. 'The worst is that his legs are infected because there is no blood circulation, so the legs are rotting and can lead to blood poisoning. Fear is that he may eat himself to death. The bottom line is that he lies in bed all the time and his mum continues to feed him with over 13,000 calories. Last time he was taken to hospital the mother continued to smuggle food, and so he did not loose any weight to allow a stomach bypass surgery that would help him change the way his stomach deals with food. Normally, after the surgery the stomach becomes smaller, and one feels satisfied with less food. Maria's challenge is to get him to do exercises and to keep to the prescribed diet. A combination of emotional therapy to deal with the addiction would be the first step before dealing with the surgery'.

Then Keisha stopped to crash the chicken bone that she held in her hand.

Soon after she said, 'this problem is a common issue, look at the streets and the kids; everyone is after fast food which is unhealthy and fatty. It has become a society problem, and instead of dealing with life threatening diseases and investing in research, money is being used in the wrong way'.

'So what is Maria's problem with the job?' questioned Danesha.

'Her biggest challenge is helping to lift him from bed so that he can wash. She is dealing with many similar cases, and it is affecting her health. Her back has become painful. When she bends it is not easy to come up. She loves her job but in a few years she may require therapy'. Keisha said.

'Is there no adult protection support to stop the mother from overfeeding the son. The young man needs to become independent to take care of himself', pondered Danesha.

As the two finished their lunch, Akan Jackson the man who helped Keisha find the job walked in. He was happy to see the two ladies and quickly invited them for a drink. His job too was unusual. He worked in a big refrigerating storage house.

'Tell Danesha where you work', coaxed Keisha. She wanted Danesha to hear for herself because she had argued endlessly

about the descriptions of his job, which sounded like he worked on the moon.

'Men! Its freezing cold! It is worse than winter! Said Akan.
Danesha looked puzzled.

'What do you mean? She was completely innocent about jobs
abroad.

'You have to wear winter gear! Full winter gear! From head
to toe!

Akan thought that he had explained enough.

'Why? Danesha could not connect winter to the store.

'We store most of the perishable goods like vegetables, meat,
fish, and even more then that it has to remain frozen all the
time even in the supermarkets. For example I work in the
frozen fish department. Before entering the store I put on a
winter coat, safety boots, gloves and a woollen hat to protect
my body from catching the cold'.

Danesha's mouth opened.

'Do you like the job? Look for something else! Keisha looked
at Akan.

'My sister you think it is that easy, life is challenging. I have
never stopped looking for my dream job. You know I am a
qualified meteorologist!' then he laughed. 'A meteorologist
in the freezing weather of the cold store! I have tried to learn
the language and I believe I am good but the conditions have
not enabled me to find one. Sometimes you are told you do
not have the qualifications or are over qualified. So that is life
here'. He turned to look at the two beauties.

Akan was interested in Keisha but she pretended not to notice.
It was her way of telling him politely that she had someone
else in her life. She did not want to hurt his feelings; she just
wanted them to remain as good friends with no love strings.

However, Akan was a man who never gave up easily; he was a gentleman who knew how to reach a woman's heart. He told jokes that send Keisha laughing and hitting him on the shoulders. Akan did not ignore this short gestures, he read too much in them. Sometimes he invited her to his friends' houses for dinner on the weekend, and took her for walks on the Danube River. As time went on he was aware of her likes and dislikes, and therefore worked within these parameters. He prayed that one day he would marry Keisha, he had began to save money towards this dream. She was the most beautiful woman and he seemed to understand why people praised women from Uganda. Akan was so carried away in his thoughts that he had forgotten about the two ladies till Keisha announced that they were leaving to prepare for the early Monday duty. She felt guilty that she had intruded on his privacy as he had a dreamy look, but they had to go.

Keisha had studied Mass Media and had a bachelor's degree before she came to Austria, but for now she was happy to take whatever came her way. She hoped that one day she would find her dream job. Before leaving she invited Akan for a beer, then paid her bill and walked out of Africa Sunshine Den.

Chapter 2

Brilliant boy

It was a warm sunny summer day as Harry arrived in Austria to join his foster parents. The sun beat down on his exposed legs. It was kind of a shock for him that the sun should be hotter here than in his country Kenya. Mrs Schmidt quickly clobbered his small legs with sun cream. He sneered, 'what is all this cream about? I mean in my country I do not need all these!' The attention was too much and irritated him. Nothing could be worse. Every time they did something for him it was followed with the words, 'poor boy, you know he is an orphan'.

Resting on the bed would be a better opportunity to get away from this mass of people who had been called to welcome him to his new home. As he looked up he noticed the bright sky against the green trees, which was wonderful. It felt magical if only he could be allowed to be on his own. A few young people had also been invited to welcome him. But he was quite shy and stood at the edge staring at the little children. At 18 years old Harry looked small for his age and would have fitted well in the group of children.

Then at that moment he imagined of how nice he could cool his body in the big swimming pool that filled the backyard; perhaps a better idea than just standing there! He dreamt of soaking himself in the cool water and floating. If only the others could jump in the pool, he would join them and then spin the ball that floated on the water, he wished!

Just as all these things were happening in his head, Mr Schmidt invited the young people to sit on the big table that was under the big chestnut tree. In his hands he held the biggest cake that Harry had ever seen in his life, but the cake did not excite him like it did with the others. Mrs Schmidt locked her arms together as she stared at Harry who did not seem to have any emotions on his face. Instead he splashed water on the small guests. The parents of these kids were unhappy but they pretended not to want to disrupt this perfect atmosphere.

'That's pretty a rough young man!' whispered one of the parents.

Mrs Schmidt tried to explain, 'Harry is a special child who sees things differently'.

One of the kids asked, 'like aliens from space!'

Then one of the parents interrupted. 'The energy inside the earth and outside is magical, and it changes with time and continues to change continually'.

Everyone was puzzled at this statement. 'What do you mean?' Asked a parent whose child had been sprayed with water. 'Are you talking to yourself or are you commenting on our new guest'.

Mrs Schmidt quickly intervened and explained. 'You see children with autism see things others see but they see it differently, that is what makes him special'. The confusion increased. Everyone's interest was awoken. It irritated Harry that now everyone was looking at him with narrowed scanning eyes, trying to find this special thing about him.

Suddenly, Harry thought about his life. In Kenya he had been the shortest boy in the class, and had a unique way of staring out of the window. Harry had created his own world and lived in it. The rest of the class thought he was mad. His parents had been killed in a car accident but Harry had survived with injuries on his head. His relatives had put him in an orphanage where they thought he could get better help because of his medical condition.

It was the mathematics teacher who had seen Harry's obvious talent in science. It had nothing to do with the accident. He was a genius and had accorded him all his attention.
'The aspects that sets him apart from the others is his ability to understand difficult concepts as well as their significance to other areas. This boy will go far'. He had predicted.
'I have taught many children in my life but I can count the number of those who were talented. I remember I taught a boy who was an absolute genius but he did not like to be called so. I only had to explain once and he did the rest. Today that boy is teaching at Harvard University! Most students did not figure out because they only learned to memorize word for word and then reproduced the same notes on the exam day. After the exam they could not remember what they had learned because they did not understand. But Harry can figure and apply, and that's what makes him brilliant!'

The debate around Harry had gone on for long because his body structure did not impress anyone. So what makes him bright?
'I would probably say that he has inherited lucky genes and an internal motivation to study! I believe that is what makes him talented and smart'.

Harry's mathematics teacher had gone on to say that what he had observed in his classroom is that there was a shared common trait among these genius kids that everything came naturally and effortlessly. Somehow, he seemed to understand that these brilliant kids could also easily get bored and even do poorly if they did not get their kind of challenging work that focus on their interest. The focus should be providing them with investigative or inquisitive topics that motivate them to seek solutions'.

The second teacher was not really convinced. 'I think that anyone can be smart if they work hard. Of course genetics, environment and effort can also determine a lot'.

Harry's mathematics teacher had gone on to argue that Harry did not need to study because he knew the subject well. 'In the beginning, I thought that he was lazy and difficult till I taught him mathematics and biology. Harry's eyes just brightened up. He was full of life. His body seemed to have increased because he sat upright and widened his shoulders. I could almost count his breathing frequencies as he sucked in everything I said. Every test I gave out he got every question right and his answers were meticulously answered! Absolutely flawless! The first time I marked his answers I was amazed because he was not the type of a serious student I knew because he never paid attention to his class teacher and never did his homework. When I gave the second test he finished even before the others could turn over the second page'.

Harry got the highest score and was the top student in the national examinations in Kenya. He had been admitted to Starehe Boys, a school that helped orphans and needy children. A family from Austria who had visited Africa Sunshine Den had heard about a project in Kenya that helped orphans find families or sponsors. Before that the Schmidts had seen their neighbours adapt an Ethiopian child and were fascinated by the idea. So when they were presented with the photo album they had selected Harry from a number of pictures. They said he had wonderful eyes that reminded one of a chameleon. Those eyes had penetrated their souls, and they had picked him. As foster parents they had sponsored his school life, and sometimes visited him. They knew he was special then; he did not say much. Only his eyes spoke about what he felt. So when he came top of the class they knew that he had a better chance if he studied in Austria, and they could also enjoy their role as foster parents. And his interest was to study pharmacy and medicine. So they had enrolled him at the University of Vienna where he began to study medicine.

Harry's ambition to study medicine was inspired by the need to help his community in Kakuma. There was neither hospital nor a clinic. Every two months the village received a group of international doctors who came in vans to treat them. Harry admired the white coats, and the stethoscopes that hang on their necks. Although he did not say anything he was allowed to touch them. These memories had stayed with him even when he moved to Nairobi to study at Starehe Boys. Then, he remembered a woman doctor who had said something like that he was autistic, a word too foreign for him. Somehow he felt it had to do with medicine, one day he would find out. This confirmed his focus to pursue medicine and to know what that word meant for his life.

So when he landed in Austria, the Schmidt family were proud of their new kid in the house. The Schmidt's did not have a child of their own but they had supported very many children from different continents. They said it was their calling by God to do so. They were proud of their good record but Harry was unique, and they were proud to show him off.

'You know he has this dark skin and little features! He has these beautifully marked eyes. Oh he is a genius!' Mrs Schmidt cooed.

So every opportunity they got they talked about him like he did not exist.

'Since he arrived he has eaten very little maybe the food is strange', said Mr Schmidt.

In fact Mr Schmidt had already made an appointment with the doctor to find out what was wrong with him. So they took him to the doctor who found everything was fine with him. Harry was not irritated instead he enjoyed the visit; it gave him an opportunity to have a close look at the practising doctor's clinic. The smile he had on his face puzzled them. He touched some of the equipment. This irritated Mrs Schmidt who apologised to the doctor many times. Her English was poor so she could not explain to Harry well that he was not supposed to touch the medical equipment in case he left germs on them. Her attempts to explain only amused him more. Then when they left the clinic he went quiet.

Harry remembers his first anatomy class like it was yesterday. It was about the human corpse. Everyone in the class had been scared. The stench had made some of the students faint; others had run off while others had given up the class. He was the only one who had moved closer. He was fascinated and his eyes brightened. Then he was allocated to a group to use the scalpel to cut the cadaver. It was in this class that he discovered his love for dissecting the cadaver to understand the human body. Harry soon got used to the environment and in fact he could locate all the different organs in the body. Surgery was like a gift in his life. Soon he developed a precision almost like a computer-programmed assistant. The professors found him exhilarating. Everyone knew that medicine was not a piece of cake and required a lot of dedication, continuous practise, and hard work. However, here was a boy who was like a magician. He did not need a second explanation. Sometimes he took up the challenge alone. Most people worked in pairs or in groups but he mastered his work alone. Harry said he concentrated better on his work when he did not experience disturbances from others. But most of his classmates did not like this attitude and tried to discourage him by saying that he lived only for the books and coffee. He did not have any friends.

In their second year, Harry became everyone's favourite because he could explain several times a topic that his colleagues did not understand. He had a gift to see things in details and to repeat many times without getting bored or giving up. It is here that the class recognised that Harry was unique, and a master of what he did. They nicknamed him 'the professor'. During the examinations he scored the best marks that left his professors surprised.

'He is too good! Sometimes they checked on his intelligence by questioning his knowledge with impromptu issues. But he answered everything almost to perfection. In fact one of his teachers was fascinated and consulted a psychologist to carry intelligent quotient tests on him so as to determine his level. They placed him above 140 on the scale for the highly gifted. The university professors and the school of medicine wanted to encourage him to stay when he finished his studies so that he could work on some interesting research topics he had proposed, which could uplift the standard of the teaching hospital on the world ranks.

Then in his last year, Harry had complained about severe headaches that he had suffered since he was a young boy but the pain was now severe. Lately the pain was blinding his vision. For the first time Harry was frightened and approached his immediate professor to seek help. Although he was shy he had to open up and explain about what he was going through. Soon after a couple of tests they discovered that he had brain tumour. The good news is that he could be operated on to remove it.

The news of the brain tumour moved Mrs Schmidt to tears. She was devastated.
'Why does he have the tumour? Poor kid, he lost his parents and now this brain tumour!'
Harry was her pride. Through him she had also studied medicine books to keep up with his knowledge. She did not want to be left out in his world. Even when he did not want conversations he had listened to her diagnose diseases of her friends and sometimes even pretended to prescribe medicine. Mr Schmidt did not understand his wife's obsession to compete with Harry's knowledge. He appreciated his brilliance and basked in the limelight when he explained to his friends what Harry was doing, and it stopped at that.

Mrs Schmidt often reminded Harry of her generosity. Sometimes she bought him oversized hoodies and trousers, huge booties and cowboy hats like she had seen young musicians wear in America. She wanted to dress him in her own liking and sometimes they clashed on tastes and style of clothing. Mr Schmidt had cautioned her to let Harry pick out his own clothes.

But she had insisted, 'what does a poor kid know about clothing styles. Let me educate him. See this is the latest in America!' Mr Schmidt could not keep up with her plots to change him. He felt sorry for Harry who watched the whole drama without a comment. This is what touched Mr Schmidt that Harry could not defend himself or offend Mrs. Schmidt.

The only things Harry had strictly kept to was food. He had refused to eat pork, Sauer Kraut and potato salad. Harry had become a vegetarian and would not listen to Mrs Schmidt pleas. Sometimes she had told her friends that he did that to spite him. But that was not true as Mr Schmidt remembered. Harry had been a poor eater right from the beginning. Anyway, now their fear was the brain tumour.

On the day of the operation Mrs Schmidt could not think right. She was a total wreck. Her heart threatened to stop. She increased her pill intake; remember she was playing the knowledgeable doctor having read medicine books to keep up with Harry the future doctor. She was delivered to the same hospital that night with an overdose of pills. Soon Harry was operated on, and recovered from surgery. Mrs Schmidt was fighting for her life on the other floor. It was only Mr Schmidt who kept the cool, and shuttled from one floor to the other to keep up with the proceedings of the two patients. The fear of losing the two most important persons in his life threatened to ruin his head. However, he discovered solace in schnapps, and he calmed his brains with it; but he over did that sometimes he forgot to make his daily visits to the hospital.

Mr Schmidt short absences did not go unnoticed because

when Mrs Schmidt recovered she asked him to recount his activities from the day she was taken to the hospital. When he failed to fill the gaps she asked the hospital staff and his best friend. Eventually, it emerged that he had failed to visit her on two days in a row because he had a blackout. Now this explained why the bar in the cellar was empty but that was not an excuse for Mrs Schmidt to start harbouring ideas that he did not love her enough. So she decided to teach him a lesson or two. Suddenly, she turned her full attention to Harry and cooked his best dishes, and slept in his room on a couch to watch over him in the night. Her total revenge plan backfired on her when Harry's professors came to visit them. She could not ignore her husband in front of people and that day she played the best wife scene in the visitors' presence. She called the husband endearing names like darling, honey, sweetheart and mouse. It was exaggerated but somehow he basked in this newfound attention. By the end of the day they had buried their battles, and could now concentrate on Harry who hated noise.

Soon Harry recovered well and he concentrated on his final year. He was a lucky boy who was studying medicine that had just saved his life. Ironically, he said it was in the operation theatre that he found peace with himself because he could concentrate, and lock out the rest of the world. It was on this same operation table that he had carried out his internship and emerged a top winner that he had been operated on. Harry was full of excitement as his graduation approached the white coat ceremony, which was going to be one of the most memorable moments in his medical school. The graduation day was a proud moment for his foster parents. Mrs Schmidt let everyone know that it was her boy wearing the white coat and taking the Hippocratic oath. She was full in her element. No one would stop her from enjoying this moment. It was her triumph.

As soon as Harry graduated he went to John Hopkins University in the USA to specialize in brain tumours. His own challenge had motivated him to pursue that line of medicine. Today he is one of the best brain surgeons thanks to his foster family. Harry also initiated a project to benefit his community in Kakuma.

Chapter 3

Bling Bling life

He entered into the unknown world. Anger from a professor had made him drop out of university where he was studying aerospace engineering. Cliff Amata was born in Banjul the capital city of Gambia. He was nineteen when he won a scholarship to study in an international university. For whatever reason he chose Austria. When he arrived he was a young man full of dreams, handsome, athletic and with a dark glittering skin. Cliff was the epitome of what African beauty stood for, and he had charisma. It was easy to notice him; he stood out like the snow on Mount Kilimanjaro. When he walked everyone thought he floated, there was a kind of lightness on his feet that exaggerated his majestic looks. He loved his African attire and ornaments, and he wore them well that they never seemed to be out of place on whichever occasion he attended. At the university he had acquired the name 'King Ras', the students loved him and only saw reggae music in him but not his intelligence.

The white women he saw and met dreamt of kissing him not on his cheeks but on his full mouth. He thought he had seen that sensuous look in their eyes. He had learned very quickly to recognise this kind of mischief in their eyes. They did not hide what they felt about him. Cliff was intrigued. The African woman always played hard to get but here there was a kind of openness about feelings that scared him but secretly he was elated. In the beginning he pretended not to be interested in their advances and dreamt of waiting to marry Mariamu his childhood crush. Although he had never confessed his love to her he knew that she too loved him.

But as a young man in Europe he had nothing to loose. The advances and temptations could not save him for Mariamu. Soon he found himself with different girls. Somehow he enjoyed seeing them fight for his love. Really, he felt like a king. He did not go after them they came after him. The partying and holidaying began to tire him when he met Karina a mature old woman who taught him so many tricks about love and sex. Karina was half polish and half Austrian; she was a self-made millionaire and lavished Cliff with everything he desired. Cliff was like a trophy and she showed him off, and enjoyed the whirlwind romance. He basked in this newfound life for the next four years. Karina bought him an expensive car, and gave him credit cards that he could use whenever and wherever he was with no limitation. She had houses in Mallorca, Tuscan and Monte Carlo. Cliff enjoyed life. The only thing that he did not enjoy was that he was drunk most of the time to keep up with Karina's lifestyle. When she had blues she drunk more and so did Cliff. Before he could recover from one hangover the next one had already begun. There were parties almost every night, which Karina claimed were related to her business.

His dreams of studying evaporated. He was narrating his life story as he sat in Africa Sunshine Den that had become his second home after leaving prison. He was trying to find his life back after spending almost ten years in jail. So after eating plantain with eggs he continued with the story as those sitting near him in the restaurant listened. Nita served him a beer, the Nigerian brand 'Star'. On this day not even Munoro the fashionable interrupted him. Babu the taxi professor observed this man with awe. Then he asked, 'Where were you before you went to jail?

Cliff looked at Babu the taxi professor and then continued.

'My life changed. When I turned twenty-five I wished to have children but Karina was at an advanced age so she did not wish to have any. I wanted to be a father at all cost. She also did not want to marry me so our arguments increased and at some point she threw me out. I was angry. I had not expected this kind of disloyalty and treatment. I had taken this to be a permanent relationship. Soon the reality caught up with me. The expensive car and credit cards were gone. Karina claimed that our love did not have any conditions; it was an open relationship that could end anytime. I was hurt. In my mind I had settled down; and all my needs had been taken care off. I had never imagined of working in my life. All the money I used to send my mother would now stop. I was full of mixed emotions where would I start?
I had quit university, I had no certificate and my scholarship had long stopped because it had been tied to my studies.
'Look at me! I may for the rest of my life not achieve something!' Cliff was scared.

Cliff remembered one of the disco owners who liked him. It was a shame that he had to plead to get a job. 'Oh manager I am at your disposal, and I can also do overtime even on the weekends. It all depends on you!' He stood there shaking, and an inner tumult threatened to explode. He had not expected to sink this low but what could he do.

Then he tried a new line of argument. 'I have a vision of

how we can improve this business and show our competitors that we are at the top, and we could also buy cheap quality goods and sell them overseas raising our profits by a big margin'. He stopped to check his performance. Had he put some intelligent points to impress the wealthy disco-owner? He wandered. 'You see if you employ me I will push the company forward! Then he remembered that he had not mentioned what kind of job he was applying for. Quickly he adjusted his voice. 'I can do anything from being an accountant, waiter, driver and personal assistant'. He ended his conversation and waited. The disco-owner unfortunately did not have a job for him but he would pass word around to his friends.

That is how Cliff entered the underworld. He had inborn leadership qualities that no other could match. The qualities he portrayed made him be loved. He quickly learned that it was important to protect each other in this part of the world and to also keep their mouth shut of whatever they did. So if he kept his mouth shut he would survive and earn his money. He was determined to rise on the hierarchical structure; he had managed to find himself a normal job as a driver to shield his criminal life and role he was now leading. When he was off duty, he dressed in expensive clothes. He said it was nice to wear expensive watches, rings and chains, and to have beautiful women and then take them on holidays in different countries. He loved the bling bling life.

Cliff sipped his beer and continued narrating. 'I quickly learned the trade and saved enough money to become a respectable businessman in the eyes of the community. With this new found money I travelled to different countries, and went into import and export business, and my business flourished, I became very powerful and bought real estate in other countries. What I noticed is that corruption is not just in Africa. Corruption is also found in Europe and elsewhere too, where everything can be bought. I witnessed shocking details and sometimes terrifying incidents in some of the countries I visited'.

Then he paused. 'I remember one day how I had been thrown out because I did not have qualifications. No one had paid attention to my Curriculum Vitae, but when I used threats people began to treat me with respect. I loved adrenalin and challenges, maybe that is what propelled me into the world of crime'. As he looked back a shadow fell over him.

'Once I travelled to my home country and landed in prison for smuggling goods. It was one of the hardest prisons in my country. I suffered brutality and slept a few hours to protect myself. There were rumours of kidnapping in prison and families were expected to pay ransoms, at worst people just disappeared. That night they tried to kill me'.

He said, 'they beat me and no tears came. Only my soul cried'.

Then I used all my money to buy protection and to save myself'.

'When I returned to Austria the police were waiting for me because my name had been tied to a drug cartel. As I was led away, I swallowed hard with my heart beating and threatening to tear apart. I had to calm myself down. I have never forgotten the facial expression of the people who saw me put in handcuffs. I remember that day, it was cold, it was dark and at first I did not know the reason why I had been arrested on arriving from my journey. In my head, I remembered how my mother had narrated about my early birth only three days ago'.

'You are a lucky boy. You know you were born too early and suffered epileptic seizures but you were full of life and survived'. Then she continued. 'The neighbours and your grandmother had given up on you, but deep down my heart I knew you had the energy to beat all odds and live. Today I thank God'.

Cliff did not understand why his mother had told him this story about his birth.

'Was it a premonition to impeding danger?' he thought.

'I looked at my talisman that hang on my neck and prayed for protection. My uncle had taken me to see a traditional medicine man, who carried out rituals to protect and save me from dangers. The medicine man had promised me that no bullets, no policeman could arrest me, and even jealous people could not harm me'.

Now he questioned this ritual. He had just arrived back only to be arrested.

'How can this happen? I am fully protected! It can only be a matter of mistake'. He convinced himself as he gazed in the distance as if he was trying to communicate with the medicine man to question what was happening now.

'As they put me in a small cell, I felt something strange like my stomach had shifted to a lower position. I knew that something bad had happened; sometimes intuition has more weight before one is confronted with evidence'.

'How would I know? I wandered.

'Can I get professional help before I say anything? I asked the officers and surely I was allowed to contact a lawyer of my choice who advised me on how to respond to the interrogation questions in their investigations.

A few days later, I was taken to court although the defence lawyers had prepared my case thoroughly, they could not save me from being sentenced to prison for drug trafficking and recruiting young people as street runners.

As I stood to be sentenced in court I felt like the light at the end of the tunnel had turned into a speeding train that threatened to crash me. I was shaken. I had never imagined that the law would catch up with me. In court as they displayed my pictures, cars, expensive attires, watches and, of people I had met, and the places I had visited, then I knew I was going to jail for a long time'. He shook his head in grief.

Cliff blamed himself. 'I think I was too comfortable with my success and ended up making mistakes. I believe I was too confident to have come back to Austria. I should have remained in Africa'. He blamed himself as he was led away to the van waiting outside to take him to jail.

As they walked towards the waiting van, Cliff asked to be escorted first to the toilets to relief himself but suddenly small things began to irritate him, and he disliked the policeman who stood next to him on the urinal as he pissed because he gave the loudest fart. He felt ashamed for this lack of privacy. Before that he would have laughed about it because it would have been among friends, now this stranger did not know about his 'wealthy' record. Here he was just a criminal not the 'chief'.

As he walked into prison that had housed many people, he did not expect a rosy life. He had heard horrifying stories about hard cores prisoners who could make life either easy or difficult.

During his first week, Cliff thought about his early life, about how he had enjoyed going out and chasing women. With his friends, they had drunk a lot of alcohol and listened to music, and engaged in a lot of nonsense behaviour that is typical of young men. When they spent many hours awake and could not go to sleep, they took sleeping tablets, and with the intake of these tablets they created a disease that did not exist by overdoing everything. They pretended to be morally upright because they wanted to conform to the world of bling bling life.

Cliff wanted to lead a life of affluence, and was afraid to be judged as poor by the wide eyes of the society he mingled with. Instead he found himself at the precipice of ruins and at the deep end of cliffs. The fear of dying poor or retiring with nothing had scared him. But now in prison he stood face to face with the reality. In the coming weeks he hid himself in his cell.

Then Cliff remembered. 'As a young boy I had dreamed a lot about becoming the first aerospace engineer in Africa with my own runaway and probably one day send spaceships to unknown planets that I strongly believed were yet to be discovered'. Cliff was a genius but he did not respect his talents or his own personality. This weakness led him to ruins. He had pushed himself to do the opposite.

'My family, relatives and community pushed me to provide them with financial support. I did not want to look in their eyes and see poverty. Instead they pushed me to find money under all circumstances. They forgot I was only human, a poor boy with humble beginnings' he lamented.

'For my family and relatives I wanted to present the image of a rich man with a generous heart. A flawless image of the successful story of the immigrant who went to Europe and found treasures and changed the life of everyone. So I did everything to fulfil this expectations and image of a millionaire with overflowing pockets of money. I was naïve and entered into a world that was not mine. Sometimes, when I did not sent enough money home my relatives talked badly of me of how I had become poor, they smeared my personality with this fabricated stories which made me depressed, and as if to prove everyone wrong I propelled myself further into the underworld. Today I know that they had trapped me with this image of a never-ending source of money. What they do not know are the many sleepless nights I spent devising plans to earn money. At times I took sleeping pills and then went on to do hard drugs but this only destroyed my mental and physical well-being.

Then when they heard that I had landed in prison they baptised me the coward and failure of the village. After the jail term I returned to my country and all I wanted was peace but my relatives did not give me any peace of mind with their continuous begging even when they knew I had lost everything. So I moved to the neighbouring countryside, where I discovered my hobby in gardening special cactus and this brought me an inner peace'. His mouth was dry and he paused.

'Then I decided to get professional help that could rehabilitate me into normalcy. It is during this therapy period that I dropped my fascination for the ruthless life I had chosen and decided to follow my ambition to study even though I was no longer young. Today I am married to my childhood love Mariamu. Thereafter I started a foundation with the help of an

41

international organisation to mentor the youth who are most vulnerable when they leave their country of origin alone and land in a wide world that has been known to swallow the majority of them'.

As we finished talking he was overwhelmed by emotions. 'My dream is that no child should be recruited into crime or violent acts of brutality, or be influenced by the bling bling life of affluence that has distracted the majority of young men from studying or following their honest dreams. It is important to maintain values and virtues that guide one. I recommend that parents should ground the upbringing of their children in a strong moral foundation that supports them in wading off false influential personalities and immoral acts'. He looked around to see if they understood his words, then he went on.

'As a father, it is heart breaking to see your own child lost, and it is hard to see anyone go through the conditions I went through. Today, in my work there are no walls or barriers that will stop me from telling the truth about life abroad. Let us preach to our villages and communities about the challenges of living abroad. Parents and relatives should not enjoy the money send to them without making serious enquiries. Life is not what it seems to be in overseas. Those in overseas should stop pretending that they live in the Garden of Eden, where money is plucked on trees, it is this encouragement that makes those back at home expect to live in royalty because they have someone abroad who can make their dreams come true. It is good to help but do not overdo it otherwise those at home will become dependent and therefore stop thinking of being responsible, and only invest in their stomachs. So do not encourage a consumer's culture. Let them invest in projects that can give them returns and good income'.

Cliff stopped talking and asked Babu the taxi professor to drive him home as we pondered about these words of wisdom.

Chapter 4

Sir Luke and life in crime

As usual on a Friday night Africa Sunshine Den was full. There was laughter till Sir Luke stood up and matched towards a group of young men his age. The situation seemed to peddle like the Swiss clock; there was electricity in the air. Everyone knew what he could do with his trained muscles. Sir Luke was soften spoken and over polite, which concealed his real character. Although he was smartly dressed he had no respect for human life. Many people whispered that he was an example of the devil. He was known to manipulate people to commit crime. Most people who knew him suspected that he was able to finance his expensive habits through tremendous huge sums of money. This particular evening there was tension as he stood towering over the young men.

What had they done to deserve this behaviour? It was like the final whistle blown before imminent danger. Nita and other customers were all standing on the table to get a better view, and then there was a crack and the table swayed as it broke into many pieces. Their heavy weight gave way and they landed on the ground. Everyone was speechless! Anger was the reaction of Sir Luke. He forgot that he had an issue with the young men. Instead he lifted Mutura who had landed near his feet with one hand. The rest of the young men saw the opportunity and organized themselves into a small group to tackle Sir Luke. Their joy was short-lived as the tragedy changed direction. He picked one by one, and opened the door and threw them all out on the road. The scene was one similar to the cowboy movies. As Sir Luke was busy dealing with the young men, Mutura used the chance to shout an insult at him in a loud voice.

'Your child is ugly that I thought you lived near the Zoo with the big Chimpanzees!

He should have known better. This was the worst remark he could have made in this circumstance. Mutura had only heard about Sir Luke but he did not know that he had just put his finger in a boiling volcano.

What happened next left everyone puzzled.

It happened so fast that no one understood how Mutura had sustained broken ribs. He lay on the floor till someone called the ambulance. As the police walked in everyone scattered. No one wanted to repeat what they had witnessed. There was jostling at the door as the guests struggled to disappear. No one opened their mouths to betray what had transpired. Sir Luke walked out and disappeared into the cold night.

Sir Luke was born in South Africa and had immigrated with his parents when he was three years old. He had a very fair complexion that he could pass for a Mulatto. As a teenage he had landed himself many times in prison as a small criminal. He had stolen in order to finance his way of dressing, and celebrated every successful incident, and spent huge sums of money. Among his circles he had shoplifted everything that he had desired. He had gone on to take orders to deliver things needed. As he grew older rumours had it that he imported stolen goods but no one could proof these rumours. Others said that he had expanded his business to include overseas territories. It was said that drug played a big role and that his partners had tricked him out. They had threatened to eradicate his family if he betrayed them. So they insisted on compensation for the protection of his family.

After that Sir Luke had become paranoid and suspected every person he saw; sometimes he harassed unsuspecting people. He suffered hallucinations, made many mistakes and eventually the law caught up with him. The system gave him a deal to leave the country, but he disappeared in the hope of reappearing but it was just a matter of time before the hand of law caught up with him. Then, the police got a tip of his hideout. They organized an early ambush and found him in bed. The search revealed the 'goods'. So he had become a liability to the country, and his fears became a reality because he had left traces of evidence that put could many people in jeopardy; it led to his arrest and deportation.

Before Christmas he was convicted of theft, peddling drugs, and blackmailing.
Protected witnesses identified him among the many people lined up as suspects. Lawyers could not save him from imprisonment nor from the final decision to deport him. They pleaded for leniency and a short-term jail, but because it was a repeated crime he would get the maximum sentence. Every crime he had committed led to a serious judgement. Finally the judge read out his judgement and convicted him.

Sir Luke had lived the 'golden period of deals' but with deportation the end had come. During the hearings what surfaced was an art of highly sophisticated communication in the world of crime that made it so perfect for him to have survived the long hand of justice. Once he was convicted he received threatening calls from his partners to stop him from 'talking' and betraying them. Just before he could deal with the calls, some detectives approached him; they wanted to know the names of his partners.

'I am afraid' trembled the muscular man.

'Tell us the names of your partners!' said the tall detective.

Before then Sir Luke had always felt strong, and would therefore threaten everyone. However, these new threats from his partners could wipe out his family. He shivered and tried to steady his upper lip that was vibrating like a palm branch on a windy day. He was confused.

What would happen to his family if he betrayed his accomplices? This question disturbed him. Sir Luke had enjoyed all the things money could buy. A heavy golden chain hang on his neck, a Rado watch glazed on his wrist and his feet were covered in a five hundred euro Nike shoe. The pair of jeans he wore revealed quality and class. Money had never been a problem for him. Only a man with money could afford this kind of expensive dressing. In a flashback, he remembered the women he had lavished with expensive outfits like fur coats, leather boots and Gucci bags. Although he did not originally like white women he had come to develope a taste for them. He treated them like toys to play with, and at any opportunity he damped them and picked the next. He said women were like buses if one bus left you waited for the next one. Word had spread around in the red-light districts about how Sir Luke spent money. They claimed that he adored women with black long hair, and that he did not negotiate for their services, he just threw bundles of money at them. In fact the majority of them had dyed their hairs black and added extensions to get a piece his of cake. Sir Luke knew that with money he could buy anything. Unfortunately, he had failed to see that these women were using him as much as he thought that he was using them.

While in his short sentimental moments he was brought back to reality by the question.

'Give us the names and you will get a fair deal'.

Sir Luke shook his head to clear his thoughts, and like a sleepy man he woke up to the reality that he faced a jail sentence and deportation.

The fear he felt before returned. Sir Luke knew, and had heard from close 'business' partners what happened to betrayers. A cold shiver ran down his spine as the officers repeated the questions in a very angry tone. The hand of justice had caught up with him.

'Give me three days to think about the real names!' He said meekly.

Sir Luke was buying time to clear his thoughts about the best way to approach and solve the dilemma. The only advantage he had is that he was from a different country unlike his partners. On second thoughts he felt safe and strong. He would definitely co-operate but he would not play the easy game. He would not release the names on first demand, he thought.

Sir Luke felt light headed once he had made up his decision. He had lied to his partners that he was from Guyana; he had never revealed his true identity to them.

All of a sudden he felt relieved and safe. Still he asked for more time. As he was led away, a small smile escaped his mouth, a short-lived triumph though. As he reached his cell he felt better. The option to be deported seemed better. He would have to prepare himself psychologically.

The sudden ambush on that fateful morning revealed that he was not smart enough like he had assumed. He had left traces of his movements, and the many places he had spent the nights. As the police broke down the door and found him in bed he was naked. He had felt embarrassed for his nakedness and pleaded to be allowed to dress quickly. As he stood in a corner huddled under the watch of dark-dressed and concealed faces, he knew the end had come.

He stood there as he witnessed his apartment being pulled apart as the officers searched for drugs and any hidden money. Every single meter in the house was searched for evidence that could connect him to a crime. Eventually, enough evidence was gathered and he was taken away.

That morning of his arrest was still fresh in his mind. He had lost everything. Only regrets and pain filled him now. Sir Luke remembered how his partners had advised him to send his money home but he did not trust anyone in his country. He had hoped to take the money with him. Now fear gripped him again.

If he were deported, where would he begin? He had nothing. The villagers would laugh and tear him apart. After living abroad for a number of years! Surely they expected him to be better, richer and knowledgeable, and on top of that have enough money to share with them.

'Life was full of contradictions'.

'Life was full of uncertainties' he whispered to himself.

In his village, Sir Luke had cultivated a progressive public image but inside himself he was cold, and this cold penetrated those who crossed his lines.

During the interrogation his true character had come to surface. The interrogators knew that he was dangerous because he showed no remorse or guilty feelings of his crimes. Recommendations were made that he should be observed in a psychiatry clinic. The observation revealed that he was psycho, a kind of neurological malfunction, who lacked emotional feelings. At times he appeared distorted and detached from reality and had an emotionless face. During the investigation when confronted with the crime he would become very aggressive. He seemed to speak to a hidden voice in his head, and other times he would turn to address an invisible person as though he was hallucinating. Other times his voice would change and he would become a very ugly angry person. He shocked the interrogators the first time these things happened as he gnashed his teeth and hit the wall.

Sir Luke had displayed a dark side of his personality for the first time when he was fifteen. He heard voices in his head but they sounded like voices outside. He said that one voice was good and seemed to comfort him but it was the bad voice that commanded him to do bad things. The first incident happened when he attacked his roommate in a boarding school but the good voice stopped him from killing him. He was so shocked by this incidence that he went to the priest to confess. Sometimes later his parents took him to a psychiatrist but Sir Luke refused to take medication. Instead he insisted that travelling to different places would be a good way of getting away from the voices, it was his best therapy. It is during these journeys that he met his first girlfriend and for her sake he took medication and the voices stopped. Then they married but when she deserted him he stopped the medication and the voices returned.

'The voice commanded me to beat and harm people, I could

not resist this inner voice because it became louder and louder. These are some of the words I heard'.

'Soon it is time!

'Here do it!

'Command him!

'After I had committed the crime, the voice would say, this
is for you!'

'Every time I beat someone the voices became low and silent, and eventually the voices would stop'. Sir Luke said.

Although he heard these voices and took their personality,
the judge summarized that he was in a position to make a
decision and decide what was right and wrong. So he was
served his sentence under observation and would continue
with therapy.

Chapter 5

Family separation

One Sunday afternoon Davina Moinina took her children for lunch to Africa Sunshine Den, she had picked them after a church service. She was an atheist but she allowed her children the freedom to worship. Davina was 39 years old and a very attractive woman who had moved with her parents to Austria as a nine year old. Her parents had originated from Sierra Leone in the late 70's. Her father worked
for an International Oil Company in Vienna, and they had led a very good life. She had attended school till age 11 when her parents separated.
Everything changed overnight.
Davina shuddered at the thought. It brought back a lot of pain. 'My mother was heart broken. My dad had been everything in her life. I recall how my mother had been a housewife; she cooked fresh meals for her family everyday, and pampered my father'. Then Davina stopped talking and looked at her children lovingly.

'Oh my mother could have gone to university; she had been very ambitious and dreamed of studying professional business management; but then she got pregnant at the age of 18 with me and married hurriedly. She was in love with my dad. Today when she describes how they met, you see this radiant look on her face, and a secretive smile appears that tells how she still feels about him. She never forgets to add that when she saw my father the first time she thought he looked like Sidney Portier, the famous American actor. To her young eyes he was the most attractive man in her town those days.

She stopped to look at her phone that was ringing.

Then she wrote a short message and continued narrating. 'My mother stayed at home to take care of her young family, while my father pursued his dreams in petroleum engineering after studying mechanical engineering at the University of Sierra Leone. During the years he was abroad my mother stayed with her in-laws who were not easy to deal with. Her mother in-law wanted her son to marry an educated woman not the village girl he left behind. Many times to spite her they encouraged the immediate neighbour's daughter whose father was a wealthy politician to begin a relationship with their son abroad. Whenever my father came back on summer holidays my mother experienced immense hatred from his family. The clothes and shoes he brought her would be taken away as soon as he left because they said she did not deserve them because she was of low status. What did she have to offer apart from the kids?, they tormented her.

Davina remembers how one day her mother was accused of adultery by her mother-in-law and who even claimed that one of the kids belonged to the neighbour.
'All these accusations and intrigues did not stop her from waiting for my father to complete his studies and come back. When he came back we moved to the big city away from the scandals and dramas of his family. Our life normalized to that of a happy family until we came to Vienna'. Davina said as she urged her children to eat Fufu, which they did not like. It had turned cold.

Then she added. 'Life suddenly changed when we got to Vienna. The big salary and the luxuries that went with my father's job changed him. He drank everyday and went to Casinos where he gambled the money. He had many girlfriends and whenever my mother confronted him he punched her like a bag of maize'.

'It is my money and you have no right to decide how I spent it' my father would shout at her.

'Who goes to work while you watch TV, and go shopping?' Thereafter he stopped giving her money for our upkeep as a punishment for mixing in his affairs.

'It was hard'. Davina whispered.

'Sometimes we went to the next-door neighbours to beg. We had nothing to eat. They found it hard to believe that a man working for such a big company could not feed his family. Anyway they were bemused but generous'. Then she continued,

'One day, I came from school and found my mother devastated. My father had decided to divorce her so that he could marry a young Russian girl that he claimed he loved. He was ready to sacrifice his family'. Davina paused and then picked at her food as she emerged from a deep thought, her appetite had disappeared.

'Today I see the tiled floor of our house where I stood as my father walked out of our lives. I was getting ready for bed when I had my mother scream. I ran down the stairs and saw my father pushing my mother against the wall. I burst into tears. I thought he would smother her as he had covered her face with a pillow. Today I do not know where I got the strength from, but I picked a small sculpture that stood in the kitchen and hit him hard on the head, then he fell with a thud'.

'Then my mother screamed. 'You have killed him! You should have let him kill me. He is our breadwinner! I looked at her'.

'What? Our breadwinner when he has already abandoned us!' I asked.

'He wanted to kill you! I was shaking at the thought. Then my father recovered from the fall.

'So you have put the children on your side to kill me! My father questioned. He left without saying another word'. 'It was the thought of our family splitting up that scared me most. Somehow I had suspected something was amiss because my father had moved to the visitor's bedroom about nine months earlier. Secretly, he had found an apartment where he took his girlfriend and he planned to move there'.

Davina ordered for more apple juice for her children and non-alcoholic beer for herself. Nita was happy to take the orders and disappeared behind the bar.

As soon as the drinks appeared Davina continued. 'But what hurt me most is that he stopped visiting us, and I remember how I wept in my bed. Somehow I was relieved that the loud shouts and fights that had increased in the last few months had stopped. It was peaceful but I was a bitter child. I missed his jolly mood and dotting love. I surely missed his presence'. She swallowed hard and saliva threatened to choke her as she coughed.

Then she added. 'The worst crime is that he neglected us; he failed to attend my twelfth birthday although my classmates had brought presents, cakes and sandwiches. My father had promised to appear but at the last minute he had called to cancel because he claimed he had another urgent appointment. For me it was not a birthday to remember even though I received a beautiful cosmetic bag. My friends tried to cheer me up. They lit up the candles on the beautiful cake but I refused to blow them off. No one understood my sorrow. The party broke up, and many years later I still blamed my father for the fault and what happened to me'. Davina brushed away the remnants of food on her daughter's face, and then asked them if they wanted to eat dessert but they declined.

So she narrated further. 'My father lived a few streets away but he did not include us in his new life. One day I visited him, and he was unhappy, and said that we had embarrassed him because of the way we had eaten. All of a sudden he thought we were dirty and uncultivated. He slapped my younger brother, and we stopped visiting him. He claimed that my brother had made the new baby cry. I remember on that day as we entered the house I had sensed that the atmosphere was different'.

At first he said. 'You cannot stay my wife's friends are coming so you have to leave now!' but we refused to leave.

Then Davina said. 'You are chasing us away, your children because of this Russian woman. All we want is to see you. Are we now an embarrassment in your new life? You do not care about us anymore?. We are not asking you to leave her we just want to be part of your life'.

'My father seemed so subdued and quiet. So we left and never visited again. That was the last time I saw my father'.

The music at the African Sunshine Den was loud and more customers were coming in to enjoy the Sunday afternoon.

Davina wanted to pay her bill and leave but Nita wanted to know what happened after she broke contact with her father. 'Now tell me, how did you manage without your dad in the picture anymore? Questioned Nita.

'It was during the summer holidays when I was 13 that I decided to visit my grandparents in Sierra Leone. My mother let my brother spent the holidays under the care of Mrs Jones our pastor's wife.

He did not like her strict discipline or the meals she cooked. At the same time Mrs Jones grumbled about my brother's uncouth behaviour; he had started stealing petty things.

I remember how one day my mother was standing on the balcony when Mrs Jones approached her about my brother. She was confused. My mother had found a job as a cleaner in a kitchen and also helped to prepare the daily dishes. Without this job I do not know how we would have survived. I remember someone advising her to take my father to court so that he could pay alimony but she declined. She would not betray her love for him, as she always insisted. Their history together was beyond the courts. Since my mother did not have any qualifications, she took up the kitchen job and sometimes ironed for people to pay our bills. She worked very hard that she had little time for us'. Davina was nostalgic and then she added.

'So the next holidays she took us to stay on a farm with her friends. We helped them to harvest grapes and I did not like it. It was on this farms that I learned about smoking all kind of things. At first it was awful but a second time, it made me relax and I forgot my troubles. I felt good. Although I did not really understand what I was doing or being told, I knew it was a cool thing to do'. Regretfully she continued.

'As a teenage I spent most of the time alone and then I discovered the gambling machines near our place. Most of my time was spent playing to finance my drug habit, and then I started sleeping with anyone who offered money. My big body structure did not betray my young age. I looked very mature.

After that everything happened very fast. I dropped out of school. My mother was horrified. She didn't want me to leave school. Amazingly my father did not say anything. The fact that he did not comment made me become aggressive.

I exploded at any little thing. Drugs now dictated my life. Many men beat me up as I tried to steal from them to maintain my new hobby.

After that I left home and moved into a small apartment without a kitchen, bathroom or even hot water. Most of the characters I came across were dreadful people when they drunk. I remember that my mother called the pastor to talk to me but I was so drunk and stoned that I did not hear what they said'. Davina shook her head in astonishment.

'It was the spring of the following year when I was 16 that I found myself pregnant. I had no school qualification or job to take care of the coming baby. Bob the father was fun to be with but he was a drug addict like me. We scouted the streets and begged for money to get the next dose. During our scouting trips on the streets we met a social worker who offered to rehabilitate us, she is the who realized that I was pregnant. I was seven months pregnant and was not aware of the consequences of my action. The social worker took me to mother-child custody institution but at night I would escape to join Bob'. Unconsciously, Davina touched her stomach and then continued.

'Then one day I was lying in bed, drowsy, suddenly I felt excruciating pain. Halfway in my pain I remembered what the doctor had said about labour pains, so I walked down the corridor. I could hear the gentle murmurs of people in the common kitchen. A few minutes later the pain increased and I screamed ugly words. I cursed Bob, my father and mother. 'I don't love you daddy! 'I don't love you mummy! 'Bob you are a stupid, idiot!' Davina smiled at the memory of her first child.

'At first these people in the kitchen ignored me because I had caused a lot of bad scenes before so I bore my pain silently, then I sensed that if I did not ask for help I might die. So I swallowed my pride and entrusted the people in the kitchen with what I was feeling. They became frightened and feared that the baby would come anytime. At first they did not know what to make of the situation. So they called the ambulance. I felt guilty for eavesdropping on them many times in the night as I planned to steal some of their things. I can still see myself standing there and holding my stomach. I remember it so clearly like it was yesterday. The ambulance arrived and as I was being taken away I could still hear raised voices, and also saw the people in the house peering through the window. Before the ambulance arrived I can still recall an old woman crying, she had never had children in her life. The same old woman visited me in the hospital the next day and advised me not to give my child away for adoption because one day I would regret. She promised to explain why she was telling me all this information'. She stopped and looked at her daughter, and touched her on the shoulders.

'So my first child Kali was born, a beautiful girl. Eight months later I had a better apartment and I ended my relationship with Bob. Our relationship was problematic and I never stopped blaming him for the baby and my new life. It was not easy being a mother at that age. At the age of 18, I recovered from drug addiction and got married. The marriage was doomed from the beginning. My new husband Heinz did not love my child and I was sorry for that. Just when I planned to divorce him I discovered that I was pregnant again. At first I was numb with shock. This new source of frustration pushed me towards cheap drugs again'. The look on Divina's face was agonizing. She continued.

'Two weeks later Heinz came from work and looked at me and said a man needs his shirts ironed and a plate of food on the table!' He went on to say things that were very emotional and hurting, and that made him look like a beast. It was the first time that we had our first fight. I honestly did not understand what he was trying to say even though he had moved out. My separation was never discussed it was a kind of physical distance that determined our parting'. Davina looked at her second daughter before continuing with the account.

'Then my second child was born Kayla a pretty girl. Heinz supported our daughter, and suddenly, we developed mutual respect for each other. Every two weeks he picked up the baby, he was a loving father and adored his daughter. When the baby was away, I took my first child to my mother and then I went partying. Soon I fell into my old habit and Heinz was not amused. He asked me to do therapy, but I ignored his advice. After talking to me to get professional help, he threatened to get the custody of the children if I did not change my ways. Thereafter, the children were taken away because I drunk and forgot to collect them from kindergarten and sometimes to feed them. The day they collected the children Heinz left me a note on the kitchen table because I was stoned and did not even notice that the kids were missing. He advised me to make arrangements to go for rehabilitation so that I could get the children back'. She almost wept as she recounted this part.

'And that was it. The children were gone. So I found time to drink, dance and enjoy. I did not feel guilty or miss them. I was permanently high, but with time I missed my youngest child. I felt like a bad mother. The anger I felt about my father had consumed me so much. I realized that my children would be traumatised through my rejection and neglect. All along I had expected my father to apologise for leaving us; but how would my children react to my negligence in future? If I felt that angry with my father for disappearing from my life, how then will my children feel? They will condemn me... Oh! It then dawned on me that my children should come first and I should not allow them to suffer any emotional stress.

Then I thought about many things. Yes, I acknowledged that I was a product of divorce and I remembered the bad memories that I still carried around even to this date. I had witnessed so much abuse in our household with my father, and the same should not happen to my children. I was gripped with frustration at this thought. Nevertheless I made a decision there and then that I would fight for the custody of my children. I also made a decision that it was time to go for rehabilitation and turn around my life. The turn around would convince the authorities to allow me to visit my children but it was easier said than done'. She stretched her legs that had almost gone numb from sitting. She went to the counter and asked for a glass of guava juice and sat down to continue with the narration.

'The effects of the drugs had affected my health. In the beginning I believed I was quite normal and all other people were crazy. I suffered short circuits of aggressive outburst. The impact on my family was frustration, helplessness, and I lacked sleep. It was difficult to make serious and reasonable decisions. However following my decision to clean up, I fought the urge to take drugs and to drink alcohol. I locked myself in the apartment though this did stop the side effects I felt. Eventually, I sought professional help. The picture of my children's picture that hang on my bed was my survival technique and motivation not to succumb and fall back to the bad habit. The drug anonymous club helped me quite a great deal. The moving stories of people struggling with hard drugs for many years, helped me realize that I would overcome this menace'. Davina smiled.

Then she continued. 'It is in these meetings that I met Fabian, a teacher whose life had disappeared in the swamp of drugs. He was so friendly, and supported my efforts to overcome. Fabian had struggled to free himself from alcohol and drugs. He had wasted his youth and energy in securing these two items. Oh! he was a highly educated man but he had lost his job because he could not control himself. Now he was in his fifties and was trying to make a career advising and supporting people with substances abuse. The first thing I realized is that Fabian did not condemn me, instead he had an understanding for the outspoken and impulsive behaviour I portrayed. His encouragement and methods saved my life. I saw the future in my own hands. Fabain encouraged me to go back to school, after all I was still young and had a bright future, and as a mother it was important that I begin my life again. Forgiveness was the first step. So it was important that

I sort and put to rest my anger towards my father'.

'One year after thorough therapy, I wrote my father a letter asking him to plan for a family meeting. I wanted to confront all my fears and rejection. I did not want to go on with life blaming others. It was time that I took control of my life, and value and appreciate myself. My ambition was to prove that I could personally get over the challenge and with the help of my family become a better person. With time I mastered my daily stress and my memory got better, and I was able to solve problems in a more reasonable manner. I would continue with rehabilitation even after the prescribed period'. Davina smiled as she talked.

'So I went back to school and trained to be a nurse to work with people struggling with substance abuse, I promised to use own my case to show that anyone can overcome these challenges. Today I am proud that I have taken control of my life, and spend time with my children. I want to be there when they wake up and when they go to bed. It is difficult to recover the years I lost in drugs but I am happy that my father has become part of life again'. Davina paid her bill and carried the remaining food home.

Chapter 6

Misshape

At first it was just a little injection here and there but after sometime the confidence grew to do more, to go under the knife to perfect her face. It had started out like a harmless correction of simple features on the upper lip, then the eyes, ears and the wrinkles.

Nick could not stop his wife Katrin from all these undertakings. He had no say. They had met on a holiday in Mombasa under interesting circumstances. He was a tour guide of the TUI Safaris; a job he loved and treasured. The relationship began after two weeks of travelling with Katrin's group. Katrin was the sweetheart in the group. She joked a lot and enjoyed dancing in the evening. So everyone liked her company, she injected a good mood in everyone, and after a couple of drinks she called each person darling. Nick found her too generous with her words. In the beginning it irritated him but soon he found out that it was just a way of referring to everyone when she could not remember their names. So he relaxed. It was Katrin who made the first moves. It excited Nick, Katrin was a very beautiful woman and very successful in her job as a hotel manager. She found Nick cool and well behaved compared to the many men she had seen in her travels.

Right from the beginning she complained of her sagging breasts, and would soon correct them before visiting him again at the coast. Nick did not see anything wrong with her breasts; she was only 35 years old and had no child. She insisted that she was not comfortable with the way they looked, and was ashamed to undress in front of him because they were not upright as she wished to have them. Nick could not stop her. Then half a year later she invited him to Austria; thereafter he discovered bumpy breast scars beneath her breasts and the misshaped nipples. He was shocked. 'I do not understand, how can a woman go to such lengths to distort her body? He thought.

'Why are you destroying your body?' Nick questioned.

Quickly, Katrin promised to do reconstruction work, words that Nick could not connect to. 'How can you reconstruct the damage? You are not a building! Finished an irritated Nick.

When Katrin had reconstructive surgery Nick was not around to witness the next disaster. He had gone back to prepare for their wedding in Kenya's Golden Beach. A few months later she arrived in Mombasa as planned, Nick did not recognize her; her lips were bulging. At first Nick thought a bee had stung her, and his family too made comments, and laughed openly. It embarrassed him that everyone was paying attention to her lips. Another noticeable change was her nose it looked smaller than he could remember. He swallowed hard, for now he decided to concentrate on their impending wedding. But in the evening as they went to their sleeping quarters, Nick approached the subject.

'Why are you changing your features? You look good the way God created you!'

Katrin could not find the right words to explain, as her English was not good enough. All the words Nick heard was, 'no confidence! big! huge! ugly!' and then she sobbed. Nick soothed her but he was unhappy with the way she worked her face muscles to produce a smile. It looked so unnatural.

The changes became apparent on their wedding day. He was embarrassed with her big sized breasts that seemed to touch her mouth. They seemed to escape from the wedding dress so that they appeared be squeezed and suffocating, and were crying out to be released from this endless cage. When he touched them they were not as he remembered them the first time. Anyway he would pretend that he was happy for the sake of peace.

After the wedding they both travelled together and had their honeymoon in Paris, the city of love, and then culminated the peak of their holiday in Venice. Nick was jealous. He did not like the way the men looked at Katrin. He felt threatened. Had it something to do with the exaggerated breasts? He wandered. For the first time he asked Katrin if she could reverse the surgery.

The question took her by surprise.

'I mean why? I like them the way they are!'

What she did not want to confess was the huge sum of money she had spent to improve her features. She could not afford a new surgery. She had already paid to have hip and buttock fat suction. This news left Nick flabbergasted. He wandered if she was crazy.

How could he explain these sudden changes on her body?

Maybe she was mentally ill he thought at first, till she started mentioning the list of prominent people who had gone on to improve their looks. For Nick this was new land.

'Is that what people did over here?' He remembered his grandmother who had such big breasts that they had made fun of them. His mother used to say that they were so big that her kids could suck them from her back. He felt amused. So many people today would admire his grandmother for having enormous breasts.

So that evening he called his mother and explained about what his wife was doing. Suddenly, screams, and more screams filled his ears.

'My son that is no woman, she is a construction. There is no warmth because these are strange things!

Next came the question that shocked him. 'How will she breastfeed your children? They will only get poison'. Then his mother began to scream again.

Nick had not thought about children. If they had them, how would they feed?' he pondered. Now he would enquire more about their future and having children.

'Had she planned to remain a dummy all her life?' he felt scared.

'Was she a water mermaid?' He jumped up from the chair and began pacing up and down.

Nick had not yet found a job and Katrin had promised that her former boss who owned a big go down would give him a job as a fork lifter because he could drive. That evening when she entered the house, he did not enquire about his job, instead he enquired about their future and children.

The discussion about their future went on till late in the night. Katrin was adamant and wanted first to travel around the world and enjoy her life before becoming a mother. Her arguments surprised him.

'I m sorry, I didn't mean to scare you!' She said looking at him lovingly.

'I don't understand what travelling around the world has to do with children!' Nick asked.

Katrin paused. Played with her fingernail and then concentrated on making the pancakes.

'You see motherhood needs planning; it is not just about setting the children in the world. We need a comfortable house, and you need a good income to raise them up. Meanwhile as we take care of these needs I want to see the world. This has been my childhood dream. After that I can settle down and focus my life on the children, but as for now I am not ready'. She turned her head towards him.

'I hope you now understand!' She finished making the last pancake and placed it on the table.

Nick wanted to remind her of the big sum she had spent on her plastic surgery but thought otherwise. It was not his money or sweat, he knew those would be the words that she would not want to hear. He felt a low-esteem as a man who was used to making decisions. Life would not be easy. Nick soon realized that he was too naïve in the ways of living abroad. He was not sure of what to do.

Eventually, Nick found a new job, and that is where he met a Kenyan who took him to the Africa Sunshine Den. It was here that he was able to ask questions about his wife's beauty. 'Is it normal for women to change their bodies by doing surgery?' Nick asked politely.

'Oh my friend that is normal and it is not a big deal' answered Maisha.

'Yes even African women do it here my brother. So it is not unique. It is the trend now to correct areas of the body one is not happy with'.

For Nick it was new territory. How could he understand? This was a strange culture.

Nick was very religious and critical of people who interfered with God's creation that was supposed to reflect His image. Would he be able to compromise his belief for his wife's body change? Anyway he ordered for his beer and walked to the corner where he joined other Africans.

Then the debate began. 'You see this man here Nick, his wife has artificial breasts, and the man is unhappy! Everyone laughed.

It irritated Nick because he thought they were laughing at him. So he paid for his beer and was about to leave when someone started a story about a Jamaican woman who wanted to her hug her boyfriend, and then one of her silicon breasts burst. This story made Nick sit down.

'What happened to the woman? he asked.

'Oh the breast just deflated, but she flew to Thailand where it was refilled' replied a man who had a French accent. Oh! It was Munoro the fashionable.

The whole group burst out. 'It is like having a petrol station to refill the cars!' and more laughter followed. The men were enjoying the discussion but Nick was worried. So he would have to treat his wife's breasts with care. Now, why all the trouble of having them when they can burst? he wandered.

Munoro the fashionable gave examples of film stars and famous people who had done plastic surgery and looked like collapsed houses. At this point Nita the waitress came to take new orders. She was experienced and knew when the customers were enjoying a discussion and therefore needed refilling quickly.

The conversation was getting interesting. 'Look at Jocelyn Wildenstein she changed her eyes and looks like a wild cat... Look at Michael Rourke, is he any better?

The fashion now is to have an African lip! So they are injecting Botox.

My brother celebrate because your lips are naturally thick'
said Munoro the fashionable; he seemed to know so much
about the ways of living abroad.

Nick was mesmerized.

Then Munoro the fashionable added. 'Today some of the
white women want to have a curvy butt like an African woman?

'What do you mean by butt? asked Nick innocently.

Munoro the fashionable looked at Nick. 'My brother do you
come from the jungle! You are too green behind the ears!
Wake up! In other words they want curves and a big buttock!' These words send everyone roaring.

'You see God gave Africans this resource for free!' interjected Maisha.

He was pacing up and down but with one ear open to the
conversations.

'We are blessed. We need to preach these to our women!
We African men are lucky but we do not take our resources
seriously', he laughed.

Nick began to relax because he now knew that what Katrin
was doing was a global phenomenon. He had heard about
how some women had developed eating disorders because
their appearance and size was very important. Of course it
was a risky health issue. Some ended up starving to death
while those who could afford used their financial ability to
have fat suction. The details of these plastic and cosmetic
surgeries frightened Nick. He recalled how Michael Jackson
had changed his colour and facial features. Yes he did not
like it! Then he said.

'What does black mean?

You know bleaching and destroying own image is like saying.

I don't like who I am

I don't like who I have become

I don't like being black

Self-expression as an African or black should not be something to be ashamed of. Africans with a complex of wanting to be white have an inferiority complex'. Then he added. 'You should see yourself as black, and as a parent strengthen your children's mentality to see themselves as blacks and to accept that as black, they can make it in life, in politics, and on the world stage'.

The immensity of the issue was bigger than he ever thought of.

Nick realized that his wife was caught up in something that was not of her creation, it was the society that had put these parameters of judging who was fat and who was thin, or deciding who was ugly and who was beautiful. These societal judgements had created insecurity in most women. The media too had used images of those women they thought were beautiful and slim. The kind of thin models put on the world runaways by big trendsetters and fashion designers had propelled even young girls to either like or hate how they looked like. The scramble for plastic surgery was an avenue to correct what they saw as anomalies in their bodies, and to fit in small sizes.

Nick remembered African cultures that once put their women in fattening houses to improve their images. Now in Austria and the world the image was a reversal. It was difficult for him to appreciate this reality. In his head he saw the notions of beauty as a relative word. Beauty depended on so many things: on the culture, country, economy, social and religious understanding.

He was deep in his philosophical thoughts when he was brought back to reality as Maisha tapped him on the shoulder.

'My brother drink your beer and leave beauty and surgeries to women!'

'Oh! What! That is not true!' interjected Mr Munoro the fashionable.

'Even men today go for plastic surgery. See my stomach, I had fat sucked out! Do you see my head? Ten years ago I started going bald and I had a young woman I wanted to impress but when she commented that my head was a reflection of how old I was I felt bad. I was only 40 and bald. I tried wearing wigs but when I drunk I forgot that I had a wig and removed it in the bar. People laughed. The worst episode is when I run for the bus and I fell, the wig flew to one side and I flew to the other. A passerby helped me up and then collected my wig, which he handed me. I was embarrassed. One day as I was still deciding what to do about my head I joined a group of people in a wedding celebration and as usual we celebrated till late. I fell asleep and then went home. Then the next day a good friend posted on Facebook my picture with the wig hanging on my face. You can imagine the comments that followed. So I decided to have hair transplantation. Yes I did hair transplantation'.

This confession raised confusion, astonishment and joy at the same time. The questions that followed send Nita the waitress running to collect new orders of beer because no one was going to leave before they got answers.

This confession stopped Nick from going home.

'Now tell us!' began Maisha, 'how did you feel? Was your stomach too heavy? What did the doctors do?'

At that moment Bwana Mkubwa appeared, and everyone shouted at him.

'Get advise from Mr Munoro the fashionable to get your big stomach small!'

Is that a greeting or an insult? Who said I wanted a small stomach?' Bwana Mkubwa went on the attack. 'Young man I am happy with the way I look! You know in Africa this is a sign of wealth and by the way women love men with big stomachs!' He waited for anyone to say something.

Then Wamaitha the African queen entered and found a panting Bwana Mkubwa.

Soon she understood what the debate was about.

'Oh dear! That is a small issue! Look I had my breasts made small, they were too big for my liking and they use to give me back pain!' Wamaitha touched her breasts with a lot of pride. 'You know after the birth of three children you do not expect them to be at full mast. So I had them corrected and tightened to make my chest look attractive'.

Nick was no longer shocked at these two confessions. This was the reality and the explanations were quite convincing, but he still wanted to hear about the hair, how would he ask without offending Mr Munoro the fashionable.

It was Bwana Mkubwa who rescued him.

'So where did the hair come from?' This question made everyone uncomfortable.

'Was it from your armpits, pubic hair or from a dead person?' They all gaped.

Mr Mkubwa had the audacity to ask such a private question but somehow they were interested.

'The hair was from the back of my head. It was cut off including the skin and then bit-by-bit planted on the areas without hair!' Mr Munoro the fashionable explained.

'Wait a moment!' Pleaded Wamaitha.

'You mean like the way we transplant seedlings to the farm!' This imagery was strong and even a weak mind now had the idea.

'Can I touch your head? asked Maisha.

Nick's eyes were wide open, and he gulped down his beer and asked for another one.

'This is very interesting' he thought.

With his fourth and fifth beer Nick knew he had to go home, he could have stayed on but he was working the next day.

As he walked out into the bright scorching sun he felt better. He was wiser. The panic he had felt before now eased and he went home a man full of hope for a happy future.

Chapter 7

My life as Au pair

As they walked down the slopes of Mount Kenya, the strong wind threatened to blow Makena off her feet. Her wind jacket was swelling, as the wind caressed her hair. She turned the other way to cover her head because her ears had turned very cold. They still had to cover 15km to reach Nanyuki, the nearest town. The scenic beauty of Mount Kenya could not be ignored from the Northern side of the central peak, which include Batian, Nelion and Lenana. That part of the mountain was drier than the other areas. So as Makena boarded the bus for Nairobi to collect her visa her feet were dusty. Only her father understood the joy that filled her heart. She felt lucky, and her dream to go abroad had finally come true. The horror stories she had heard about au pairs in Europe would not stop her from her chance to travel and study the German language that she had started in school. Makena had clear ambitions; she hoped that one day she would open her own college and teach standard German language.

Therefore as soon as she finished high school she had combed the Internet to find a host family that could accept her as au pair. Luckily, she came across a family in Austria that fitted her expectations. So she took the opportunity because she had some experience with children and her own siblings.

Makena continued to narrate her story as she chatted with Rushell another au pair girl from Kenya she had met at the Vienna International Church.

'When I arrived in Austria, I knew I had made the right choice. The host family met me at the airport with their three young kids'. Makena smiled. 'I enjoyed the rid home to Baden, a small town. What a day! My first experience abroad! I just sat in the car and could hardly believe the many beautiful places I saw. Coming from Nyanyuki the big streets and the magnitude of lights was overwhelming.

We then got to the house and the little kids led me to my room. It had a big bed, a shower, a big balcony and a TV with Internet access. I was excited and thrilled to have such a beautiful room to myself. As I was still exclaiming at the beauty of my room, the family asked me to join them for supper'. Makena then walked to the ladies toilets to clean her hands after eating lamb ribs.

Makena remembers, 'I was the first black person in their lives. The children had never been close to a black person before and were curious. That night as we walked downstairs to eat supper one of the kids approached me'.

'You did not wash your hands clean! said Lisa the eldest child who was about seven. 'Then she rubbed my hands vigorously,' Makena said.

'Come follow me to the sink and I will show you the soap,' added Lisa as she held my hand tightly and led the way to the sink that was in the bathroom.

In the bathroom Lisa took the hand soap and poured so much on my hands and asked me to scrub hard which I did'.

Then after sometime she said. 'But they are still dirty!' She was disappointed.

'Oh it then dawned on me. She was puzzled about my colour. So I explained that my hands were not dirty; that was my colour. Still she was not convinced and as we walked into the living I explained Lisa's puzzle to her parents. I do not understand why they apologized. Lisa was trying to understand why my hands were different, and I was happy to explain to her about black people and colour. Then I stopped talking to the relief of the parents'.

Suddenly, Alex the second born forgot his shyness and made his first move.

'Can I touch your hair? Why is it like this?

'I braided it. Next time I will show you how I do it,' said Makena as she filled her plate with food.

'Now kids eat! Let Makena rest, you know she has had a long journey,' whispered Mrs Weber. Her words only seemed to increase their curiosity, and then I told her to let them ask so that they could feel free with me. Some questions made me laugh.

'Do you live in a house like ours? Is the flying Jumbo your friend? Oh is the Lion King in Kenya! I cannot recall who asked what. By the time supper was over the smallest member Diana was sitting on my laps very comfortable, and inspecting my teeth, ears and eyes. She had this fascinating look of innocence that warmed my heart. I felt touched and loved. The kids escorted me to my room and wanted to sleep on my bed. They were all competing for attention.'

The next day my host family got me enrolled in 'Volkschule' a kind of community school for German classes that I could attend as the children went to Kindergarten. Both parents were doctors in the main hospital, and worked on similar shifts. They treated me with a lot of respect and gave me a welcoming package, surely they left a fantastic impression on me, and I was motivated to work. On the weekends we spent lovely weekends in their country house in Burgenland and sometimes made trips to the neighbouring countries, Italy, German, France and Switzerland'.

Then winter came. 'Oh! Snow! For the first time I was covered with snow from my head to my legs as I picked the kids from kindergarten. The Weber's bought me a winter jacket and boots but the feeling was thrilling. Touching snow and playing with the kids outside was wonderful. What a marvellous form of precipitation! I had only seen in movies house with decorations and lighting techniques during Christmas, but now I was experiencing it, I was left speechless. Then one of my young neighbours invited me to join her to visit the Christmas market when I was free. I even had the opportunity to accompany her for a short drive in Sopron in Hungary for a Christmas concert. What an unforgettable experience that was! Over summer in the coming year I visited Warsaw and Amsterdam. My host family gave me days off to go after my hobby, which was travelling and making new friends. I can say that socially, I managed to make many friends even though the culture and countries were new to me'.

Then Rushell asked, 'what about you daily chore in the household? Makena played with her glass of water before replying.
'Mrs Weber had given me a free hand on how I wanted to do the house chore. There was no fixed routine. After taking the kids to Kindergarten, I went for my German classes; sometimes I would clean the house if I thought it was dirty. I did laundry everyday maybe a habit I had from Kenya to wash clothes everyday. Once a week I did all the ironing and changed beddings. On a daily bases I dusted the shelves, windows, and any other place where dust could settle. One of the kids had a strong allergy against dust. Then I cooked before picking the kids from school. The children loved the

playgrounds and so I took them there before coming home to read both English and German books. Sometimes I taught them rhymes. I remember the day I taught them a Swahili song, and asked them to sing for their dad on his birthday. I can still see Mr Weber cleaning his nose with gratitude. He hugged me and could not find words to express what he felt. My biggest challenge was baking, I produced what I could and the kids enjoyed the figureless or misshaped cakes but they did not criticize me, they only said I was improving with every cake I made. I am not sure if they wanted to make me happy but I believed them. I am not an expert in baking. Then the most memorable time was sleighing in the winter. It is an activity that captured my attention and encouraged me to try skiing.' Makena looked at Rushell as Nita the waitress joined them on their table as soon as she heard about skiing.

Nita questioned, 'you mean you can ski? Really! You are the first black woman I have heard who enjoys skiing?'

Makena took up the challenge. 'It was not easy it was a very difficult experience. So I joined the kids. Lisa and Alex were good they were patient with me; they held my hands and encouraged me. They got very scared the first time I fell. They thought that I had broken every bone in my body because the impact of the fall sent a few snowflakes flying in the air. Of course I was hurt but I played cool and brave. When I got home my back and knee was hurting. So the next morning I stayed at home with the excuse of catching up with ironing clothes. The next time I made a few moves, and soon found myself zigzagging on the ski piste. By the end of the third week I rolled down the slope as a professional skier. The

Weber's were proud of my performance and ability to try out everything. That is how I discovered my love for skiing.' Makena stopped.

Rushell opened her mouth in awe. 'You are marvellous. You amaze me. How do you manage all this? No wonder the Weber's love you like a daughter. You know my host family is okay but they are not adventurous. They love to watch TV and grill in the garden but they do entertain quite a lot. They have a small disco in the cellar and on the weekends they spent time down there. The house is big and has a pool in the basement, and a modern Jacuzzi. I can say that they are nice people and always include me in their entertainment program. The only problem I have is when I have to repeat my personal story, and then everyone tries to look at me as a fragile person. Sometimes the women bring me their second hand clothes or articles. I have learned to select the good ones, and then take the rest to the Caritas' collecting areas. I am happy and when I compare myself to the stories I hear about the au pairs in Middle East I feel lucky'. She asked Nita to bring her a glass of red wine. It was her free day and intended to enjoy before going to a disco.

'What have you heard about au pairs in Middle East? asked Makena.
'Mmh! Very bad stories from a Philippine that just moved to Vienna from Lebanon. She recalls how her boss took away her documents on the first day. After that it was cruelty that filled her days. She woke up at four and began washing, then cooked breakfast, cleaned the 18-roomed house without a break. At 12 o'clock joined the women in the kitchen to cook lunch. When everybody else had eaten she was asked to eat

remnants and then washed the endless dishes. The afternoon was spent cooking dinner for the big family, washing the kids, and serving coffee to the men who sat in the living room. At about midnight she would eat what was left and then crawl into bed; but it was the beatings and wounds inflicted on her body that made her escape. After working for two years she received no salary. She was so disappointed but it was not the money that depressed her most it was the cruelty that she experienced. So she risked her life and left, she knew that anytime someone was caught fleeing they would say one was a thief and had stolen valuables. However, the fear of such accusations and going to jail did not stop her from fleeing. ' Rushell touched Makena on her face and stopped talking. Then Eva another Kenyan joined them, she was an au pair now living with a second family.

Makena said, 'I think we are lucky I met Eva in the church'. Eva tell us your story cajoled Makena.

'I am from Lamu and 19 years old, and I suffered at the hands of my first host family. I found the family on the Internet, and they liked my profile and after that we talked on Skype. After a while the family contacted me so that we could discuss before engaging me. They wanted to know and understand what my own expectations were as an au pair, and also to find out if I knew what my duties would be'. She held her handbag as if seeking for comfort.

Then Eva continued, 'on Skype everything worked out well, and my impression was very good. I learned that my host family would pay for my German classes, daily fare, refund my flight cost, and give me the agreed salary. The formalities were completed and I would begin my work at the beginning of the year. One thing I remember I did not do was to sign a contract, maybe they had overseen this task,' thought Eva.

'So what happened?' inquired Makena.

Eva continued. 'When I arrived I was a bit confused, the host family just exchanged a few words with me. I mean on Skype they were friendly and joked a lot. It was funny that they were not curious or inquisitive. The first day they left early, and I took the kids to school, which was not far. Then I did the house chores that we had discussed. Most times they were gone the whole day and arrived around eight in the evening, ate and put the kids to bed and disappeared. The next thing the father gave me a credit card in his name, which was a puzzle. I did not understand what that meant. After a month, I asked myself if everything was okay? They had not commented about my work, the food I cooked or about the kids who cried all the time'. She stopped talking and looked at Makena sorrowfully.

'Why would they give you a credit for your private use?' questioned Makena shaking her head.

'Then I fell sick that is when I knew that they had not insured me. My host family panicked? continued Eva. 'I had fever. Mrs Muller bought some on-the-counter medication and lamented how expensive it was to see a doctor. I did not complain but they did not allow me to lie down. What hurt me most is that I had to cook and iron. I had been on my feet for more than 12 hours and did not have energy. I remember how she sent the kids to ask me to serve them food. The next morning they left without asking if I was feeling better. This was my first bad flu and did not know what to do. I almost crawled as I took the Kids to school that day. My head drummed and pounded like a motor. Even the teachers commented about my flu and asked me to stay away from the other kids in case I infected them. Soon after, they rang Mrs

Muller about my condition but she only scolded me. I felt lost because sometimes they came late and never informed me of anything. It was getting unbearable?' Eva remarked.

Makena seemed shocked. 'You mean there are such host families? Mine is like my own family!

Eva continued. 'Then the surprise came. They began to complain about everything I did. The floor has not been cleaned well; my underwear and socks have not been ironed. Suddenly their attitude changed. The host family found mistakes in everything I did. The worst thing is that I heard them talk ill of me and they stopped appreciating my efforts in bringing the kids to understand table manners and being polite to people. Soon I was asked to prepare my own food, and to wash my clothes separately, to buy my own bathing soap, I was made to understand where I was suppose to sit and even when to answer the phone. The attitude towards me wasn't positive at all. I was now a mere worker and not part of the home,' completed Eva

Makena made her face small. 'How can you persevere such mistreatment? Why did you not talk to them or complain about such behaviour?'

'One day I confronted Mrs Muller, and do you know what she said'. Eva gave a dry laugh.

'I never asked you to do all the housework; you said you knew what is expected of you as an au pair on Skype'. Mrs Muller looked triumphant. 'You misunderstood! The uncomfortable atmosphere is your own imagination! Mrs Muller finished and walked away dragging her high-heels that put extra holes in the wooden floor.

'Unbelievable! screamed Eva. 'This family is taking advantage of me'.

Immediately then Mr Muller appeared and told me, 'you have made my wife unhappy!'

'Did I hear right? Me Eva making your wife unhappy! I knew better than that. I would have to leave. 'Sorry but I am leaving! Eva licked her lips as she finished the sentence.

'Mr Muller stood there with a motionless face as I boarded the bus back to stay with a fellow Kenyan in Vienna. That night I felt happy. I remember how Mr Muller stared at me with a cold calculating stare as I carried my belongings out. He deducted the fee for German classes and fare to the courses although they had promised to pay. You know I had their emails and could prove that but because I wanted peace of mind I left. The next morning he called my family in Kenya and pretended to be shocked about my going away. He said that I was lying about his wife because she was a kind-hearted person'. Eva was amazed.

Then Eva spoke to him. 'Oh you have forgotten how your wife locked me out at eight in the evening on my free day, and I could not open the door even when I had the key. How many nights have I slept outside the door? Countless! In the last few days she has stopped responding to my greetings, and her tone has become rude. Have you forgotten your wife saying I am increasing your cost when I make pancakes for the children, a meal they like' Eva said.

'Today, I live with a wonderful family who care about me and are encouraging me to pursue bachelor studies at the University of Vienna. I am quite happy that is why I am able to meet you people here in Africa Sunshine Den. Sometimes they even allow me to invite my Austrian boyfriend home on special occasions. The best time was when they celebrated my birthday. I felt honoured,' completed Eva.

'I have heard many stories but I cannot imagine because my own experience is wonderful'. Makena sympathized with Eva but at the same time felt happy for her for the new nice family.

Chapter 8

Mrs Sunny the teacher

Aileen was a young little girl sitting at a small desk near the window, but she didn't notice the teacher enter the class. She didn't see that the other children had moved to the big table set for communication activities. She didn't see the happy children. They were laughing and having fun. She was so engrossed in her own thoughts. She was staring at the wall next to her small cupboard with such interest that she didn't notice the teacher standing next to her.

'Aileen, you should move to the big table,' commanded the teacher.

'I'm sorry,' she apologized to Mrs Sunny. She didn't seem happy to be interrupted in a world that she had created for herself.

'Could you stand up now!' the teacher insisted.

Aileen just stared without responding. She began to breath loudly. She opened her eyes wider. She pulled her hands from her small pockets and banged her desk.

' No way!' she shouted. Her nostrils let out hot air.

'I am sitting here!' finally she said.

Aileen walked to the corner of the room and sat down in the well laid out carpet. She threw things around, and at the boys sitting at the far edge. She picked up a small mirror and looked at her face, then touched her hair that had been stalked up in one big bundle. Then a small smile appeared on her face. It was a triumph smile Aileen had gotten her way to do what she wanted to do.

With disappointment Mrs Sunny walked back to her big table where the other kids were waiting patiently. Then she picked up the book she knew by heart. She didn't want to interfere with the children's happy mood because they were playing intensely. The clang of joy filled the classroom. This did not distract Aileen's self- made world. Aileen had picked up a fairy tale book, and was opening page by page without reading. The flapping of the pages was so loud. When no one paid attention to her she banged the book so hard on the floor and with a big smile she looked around and wrote her name with big markers on the cupboard.

Mrs Sunny walked to where she stood, and patiently asked her to stop.

'You are ruining the cupboard with colour!'

Aileen stared back, and picked a pair of scissors and cut her dress.

Mrs Sunny took the scissors away, and asked her if she wanted to do the activities with the other kids.

Aileen silently walked to the big table. She began to speak words that no one understood. Then she sat next to Diamond. 'Here is a card for you?' he said. Aileen picked up the card and began to paint it in pink. She used so much energy to colour it that Mrs Sunny shouted,

'Stop! You are supposed to put the card next to the picture'.

'I love to colour,' said Aileen.

'The activity is not to colour,' said Mrs Sunny.

She loved Aileen; she was a special child and required a lot of attention.

Aileen loved to sit there for hours watching the other kids;

the thing she liked was to play with the keyboard and computer. When she touched the keyboard, her small fingers came alive. They raced down on the keys. She was a very talented child. Music seemed to calm her down, and all her energy was put into creating tones that she had in her vision. Immediately, the kids paid attention to her clang, it sounded so dramatic that Diamond her closet friend smiled.

'Sounds like that track in the movie Titanic.'

Then all the kids surrounded her and she blossomed in their little stares. Yes, this is what she loved; attention and recognition, and as if to proof them right she played the next number. It was wonderful and when she completed the whole class clapped.

As the children clapped Mrs Sunny remembered her own teachers in Kenya. They would have dealt with Aileen differently. In her days as a young girl, the morning assemblies were used for announcements but also to discipline noisemakers, disruptive, and difficult children. The belief then was to beat them so that they could listen. Today she knows that the noisemakers would have been children with specials needs that were termed as 'Kichwa Ngumu' (headstrong or stubborn). Maybe some of them had Attention Deficiency Hyperactive Syndrome (ADHS) but it was downplayed. Some were termed as 'Mjinga kama baba yako' (stupid like your father) because they were poor and slow in certain subjects. Therefore, teachers failed to appreciate that when children did not understand a subject, they were not necessarily idiots or morons. Some of the children may have been interested in other things. Some were highly gifted in other areas but these qualities were not recognized and supported. The teachers were not sympathetic, and punishment was meted out accordingly. It was common to find the same children being caned everyday but the punishment did not deter them from making noise and being disruptive.

Mrs Sunny shook her head as she thought of how they could have diverted this energy into positive and productive use by providing music, painting, drama and other skills. She then recalled Mary Njena who was a very shy and quiet student. She kept to herself and rarely said a word. She was happy to be on her own but the class teacher always wrote in her report card that she was anti-social, and was also poor in conversations. Today Mrs Sunny knows that Mary was a very special child with autistic characteristic, and did not experience the love of a teacher or the joy of being in a school.

Then there was another child, Wamahiu, who was branded as hotheaded, rude, a fighter, impossible to deal with, and the school would not keep him. They said that he challenged and threatened every teacher. Today, Mrs Sunny knows that it was puberty and too much testosterone that had a strong impact on him. He just wanted to be recognized as the strongest and so he dared everyone. Eventually, he dropped out of school because he could not keep up with the caning. He was just a bully looking for recognition and attention.

As Mrs Sunny controlled the drawing activity the kids were doing she recalled how some of the children in her primary school were put in approved schools as small criminals, and sometimes termed as kids with madness. As she continued to turn these thoughts in her head of what would have been the best approach, she saw Julian a young boy who wore certain specific clothes on different days of the week. He bit his nails as he looked at the calendar, speaking to himself.

'I hate Saturdays,' he said as he flipped through the colour-coded book on his desk making sure that he had everything ready for the next lesson. Next he turned to Diamond who was sitting next to him and mentioned the colour of the clothes he would wear the next day. Mrs Sunny turned to him as she asked Diamond to finish his assignment so that she could listen to Julian who had gone on with the narration.

'Blue shirt on Monday
 Red t-shirt for Tuesday
White hoodie for Wednesday
Green cotton shirt for Thursday
And purple snickers for Friday'

Mrs Sunny knew Julian's behaviour was not madness. He just needed empathy and understanding. She respected his choice of colours as she also patiently listened to his explanation about his sister's choice of colour he was supposed to wear to the kid's dance. She had insisted that he wears pink, a colour he really disliked.

Julian was afraid of the other kids and treated most of them with indifference. Although his eyes were kind, he was a loner who preferred to spend his time reading Harry Porter. He ignored every teacher's advice to put away the books away till after the classes or to leave them at home.

Mrs Sunny had found a compromising strategy.

'Julian if you put away that book I will give you ten minutes extra to read the book after you have adequately completed the assignment.' This strategy worked. Every day, Julian would quickly finish his allocated task without using abusive words or challenging the teacher. Sometimes he got a sticker or a bonus point for cooperating with Mrs Sunny. He enjoyed her lessons because she had managed to turn his challenging behaviour into positive.

Mrs Sunny had been able to read Julian's actions as a cry for recognition. Her strategy worked very well in enabling him adapt satisfactorily to the class activities.

'All kids are different. Some are brilliant, some are unmotivated and stubborn, and if they do not like a subject they talk of how they hate coming to school', commented Mrs Sunny to her assistant.

She also remembered the most frequent phrases used in the teachers' vocabulary: disrespectful, a problem child. These tags do not help solve the problem. It is important to identify the real cause of the challenging behaviour.

Mrs Sunny felt that to minimise the problems it was important to see that the kids were able to adapt well. From her many years of teaching she knew that most children portrayed challenging behaviour when they were unable to cope with a situation. So teachers needed to develop coping mechanisms for these children like working out collaborating solutions; showing empathy and reminding them continuously on agreed classroom strategies. Most of all it is important to find out and understand how each child learns.

The bright sun blinded the pupils working on the table next to the window, so she walked to window and pulled the shutters down.

Mrs Sunny spoke to her assistant, 'You know punishment

and coercion should be replaced by reinforcing good behaviour, teaching life changing skills and using technology.' The assistant looked at her.

'Many times rewarding co-operative behaviour and creating a competitive atmosphere maybe even push them to work in teams,' said the teacher assistant.

Then the teacher assistant narrated how it had been difficult to take over the class from the previous teacher because the children had complained that they did not understand the instructions. As soon Mrs Sunny took over the class and she did not utter a word, instead she wrote on the board the book page number of the task, and then rewarded the person who was the fastest to open the page.

Then she went on to turn many classroom activities into a competition. It worked but not for all of them although there was a new dynamism in the class. The children enjoyed.

It was only Johnny, who was slow and could not keep up. So he protested, cried, and threw things around.

'They are mean and yet they get all the stickers!' he complained

At first this new conflict left Mrs Sunny overwhelmed and she quickly searched her brains for new ways to cope with the new challenge.

Johnny was right to feel left out. She had to devise a way of including him in the competition. She gave him simple activities that he could master for his level. This approach seemed to work very well. Johnny was thrilled to get a sticker. His eyes glazed as he showed off his sticker.

Then she remembered her class teacher in her days in Kenya,

who used to write their names on the board for noise making or any other behavioural challenges they got involved with in the class. If someone's name appeared many times on the board they were asked to see the discipline master. Mostly, the children did not like having their names written on the board. The approach may have had some positive impact on some of the pupils' behaviour but not on Ojwang who went out of his way to beat the school system by devising disruptive behaviour to revenge on the teachers. It was like a ceremony when he was asked to see the discipline master because everyone saw him as the sacrificial lamb. They admired his courage and brevity to be walking to that 'feared' office. After receiving the 'Treatment' as they called it, he would demonstrate how he held the teacher's hand, and how strong he had been to challenge the teachers. These accounts increased his popularity in the school. It was said that it required five teachers to pin him down in order to cane him. They thought that he had magical powers to overcome them.

'Teacher, what have I done?' was the most used statement when he walked to the dreaded office!

Today Mrs Sunny knows that rewarding Ojwang's good behaviour would have had a better outcome than punishing his bad behaviour. Of course some of these strategies may not work with all children.

As she went home after work, she remembered an incident that still sends cold shivers down her spine. Peter Finegold had been a student in the school she first taught upon her completion of Masters degree in Vienna. Finegold was about fifteen years in his final year before going to a commercial school. He seemed to have liked her so much. He said to her,

'I enjoy being in your class, you are patient, tolerant and treat everyone equally.' Mrs Sunny was touched by these kind remarks from Finegold. This kind of feedback made her appreciate her choice to be a teacher.

Unfortunately Finegold had suffered degradation among his peer because of his 'big breasts' on the chest. On the surface he was an average student but his performance had deteriorated. Sometimes he failed to attend school, and eventually he became aggressive and argued a lot; he also quarrelled very often and looked for fights. It is during one of the school trips that he revealed his true character when he molested a girl. At first everyone was shocked. No one had expected him to show that kind of hatred he was harbouring inside himself. It was obvious that he hated women, but this one incident was not enough to pass a final judgement.

In the last semester he chose to do a presentation on sharks. In his explanations there were elements of sadism. This did not deter anyone from listening and clapping when he finally finished. However, a strange feeling overcame everyone in the class, and in their mind they thought his behaviour was weird especially when they celebrated their last day in school. Mrs Sunny remembers some of his peers saying that it is like he had two faces; that of a monster or a raging bull but also a calm loving side. These characteristics were not so apparent even as he left school.

When he completed his training he fell in love with a Kindergarten friend, they had fun and enjoyed life together, and at some point got married. Finegold was the most loving husband till he had an accident that changed his life. He had a brain injury that changed him. Finegold developed mood swings; aggressive out bursts, and fights. He beat his wife whenever he felt provoked. She ended up in hospital suffering from his severe beatings.

'Not in a million years would I have thought that we would be inseparable!' said Mrs Feingold.

Naturally, the divorce followed. This separation awoke a deep anger that consumed him. He became obsessive; he could not live without his wife and began to follow her everywhere. After a couple of months this anger exploded and he attacked his former wife. He beat her so bad and then left her for the dead. She never recovered from the beating. She died of serious injuries.

The image and memories that Mrs Sunny had of Finegold is that he was a fine gentleman who was polite and helpful. She struggled to search her mind for any signs that would betray that kind of brutality. She then remembered the few comments from his classmates and she felt guilty. Would she have helped to change him? This question weighted on her mind.

Had the school failed in some ways for failing to listen to the students' comments about his sometimes-unusual behaviour?

Mrs Sunny went to the courts to listen to Finegold case. Here, she witnessed a young man who showed no remorse, and was cold and seemed completely oblivious of the events and noise around him. The descriptions of Finegold's accusations shocked her. The many rape cases that had been reported were traced back to him. Everyone who heard about his demented severe sexual drive was left breathless.

What had gone wrong? This dark side of his personality had remained hidden.

However Mrs. Sunny remembers that Finegold was a loner and preferred to master his activities without group work; but she also remembered that he had a difficult childhood. His step-father had traumatised him, always calling him a looser. He had also been bullied in school for his 'big breasts' a medical anomaly.

Mr Sunny sat there and knew that the system had failed to protect Finegold, and to help him deal with his physical and psychological dilemmas. As she walked out of the court she prayed for Finegold to be given a chance to undergo psycho-therapy treatment. She realized that there was still a lot she needed to understand about human personality. Her focus would be to delve deeper into psychology especially emotional development and mental wellbeing.

Once outside on the streets she noted that the sky had turned grey. She entertained the thought of going back into the court buildings but before she could make the move, she saw the dark swirling mass of sky-water reaching her on the street. The sun had disappeared behind large ashen clouds that were looming on the horizon. She quickly looked for her car that she had parked across the main street. She got into the car and pulled away. The traffic was slow almost at a creeping tempo as everyone hurried to get out of the city. She got to her gate, and then jumped out. The first drops of rain hit her like a whip. The drops penetrated her thin blouse as she struggled to find the keys in her handbag. After a while she found the key and pushed the door open. She was dripping, and as she walked into the house she left a trail of water on the marble floor. She was wet and breathing hard. The combination of her body heat and the cold began to dissipate. Her skin got goose bumps and she trembled. Quickly she climbed the wooden stairs and disappeared into her bedroom where she changed into warm clothes. Then she made a hot cup of green tea and climbed into her bed. She switched on a small stereo that stood on a small drawer next to the bed. The melancholic song matched her dull mood, and then began to read a journal on educational essentialism and existentialism. As she read she lay back and did not care about the sudden darkness that had set in. Then the loud thunder that vibrated across the house made her curl up under the thick duvet. Although she was over forty years, she could not hide her fear especially when the lightning brightened the room.

It then got darker. This darkness seemed to reflect how she felt but the perpetual flowing rain made her feel drowsy. Then thoughts of her students filled her head. She thought of Fabian who had almost had a breakdown because he was afraid to take poor marks home. The boy had wept uncontrollably because he was terrified of his mother who could not accept that her son could not achieve the best mark. Fabian had pleaded with the teacher to give him a better mark but she could not do it. It was his ability that she had tested and she could not just reward him for a performance he could not produce. That would be a lie and lack of integrity. Mrs Sunny could not understand parents who pushed their kids beyond their abilities, and therefore instilled fear or hatred for school. Fabian was not the only case. She had heard other teachers too complain about the art of 'begging' for marks.

It was deeply depressing. The children just aimed to pass exams and reproduce what had been taught. The children's well-being and humanity had remained somewhere on the track as the world measured people according to their school performance based on a note system. She then recalled the news of the national examination results in Kenya, where schools results had been cancelled for serious cases of cheating. Something had gone wrong with the education system in the whole world. The systems focused and supported an exam-oriented culture that forgot about character building and integrity so that it produced half-baked citizens.

Then Mrs Sunny's husband walked in, and turned on the lights, this unbearable brightness hurt her eyes and brought her out of her reverie. For the moment she had to surrender her sanctuary as she joined him for dinner at Africa Sunshine Den, at least she would not endure the rainy day alone. When they came back she read her pupils' work and prepared the end of term report. Mrs Sunny lost track of the rain outside, as she got lost in her thoughts again.

She had studied for a bachelor degree in education in Kenya and had come to Austria to do her Masters. Although she had taught for six years in Kenya, the University of Vienna had required her to do more hours in psychology, history of education and philosophy as bridging courses before embarking on her Masters study. The University's system of calculating and transferring notes meant that it was like re-doing the bachelor level again. It would take her about four years to complete her educational course and teaching subjects. To be able to teach in Austria she was also required to do a teaching practice. So in her last year of her course she specialized in special education, and had the opportunity to work while she planned to pursue a Ph.D degree

So as she taught in class she was able to compare the challenges of learning in Austria and Kenya. She realized that the education system in Kenya needed to improve more in providing adequate learning resources, technology, and to have small numbers of pupils in the classroom that were manageable. There was also a need to identify talents in kids as early as possible, and support the development of these talents. An increase in the school budget, and responsible policy-makers could make a difference in providing quality education. It seemed to her that there was an urgency to increase the number of teaching personnel in the class, and to create positions of support staff and social workers to assist the teachers in primary school. She also reflected on the need to make guidance and counselling management active in dealing with youth challenges in high schools. In Austria she felt that the parents should take a serious role in the emotional development of their kids, and also monitor what the kids watched on social media, and the kind of peer groups they joined.

That night she went to bed determined to help change or at least influence a change of the mindset of the policy-makers in both countries.

Chapter 9

My children

Janerose stooped and kissed her youngest child Tanisha who was six years old. She was a very beautiful woman with tattoos all round her neck. It was the missing front teeth that made her look hard. She loved to wear black especially leather trousers, and jacket, and high boots. Most of the women who saw her were afraid, and had this feeling that something was amiss. Janerose was born in Northern Uganda and came to Austria when she was 20 years old. The harsh circumstances in her environment had turned Janerose into a rebellious young girl. The insurgency of the Lord's Resistant Army (LRA) led by Joseph Kony had produced a lot of great suffering and horrific atrocities for the many displaced people in Uganda. Janerose was abducted to become a fighter and ended up becoming a sex slave at the age of 13 years. To save herself from the many cruel encounters with men she went to live with a boyfriend in the camp who had sympathised with her situation, and offered her protection. So she matured quickly.

At 14 year old she began to experiment with cigarettes and alcohol, most of the time she was high from the cheap marijuana joints that they were given so that they could carry out heinous attacks. At 15 she had her first child, then at sixteen the next one was born, finally she married her boyfriend and settled down. Life did not go the way she had expected. The young husband had no sense of responsibility for his young family. He used his little money on alcohol and cheap smoking joints and when he smoked these joints he terrorized the family. Suddenly, life had become a nightmare and it did not seem to get any better. At seventeen Janerose had no choice but to leave, she had to fend for herself. With a few coins in her pockets she moved to Lira town. She had no idea where she would begin but she felt in her innermost self that she would be able to support her children. She made a pledge to take any job that came her way.

On the first day she approached the church mission to provide her with accommodation till she was able to find a place of her own. She had no relatives and knew no one. As luck would be on her side, an elderly church member agreed to take her in, this woman had lost her entire family, she did not have a big house but Janesrose could sleep in the kitchen with her children. Soon Janerose found a job as a waiter in a small community restaurant. It was run by the church and offered descent meals to tourists or visitors working for non-governmental organizations. The job did not pay much but she was able to buy the daily provisions for her kids. Her kids stayed home with their new grandmother and loved her because she spoiled them. It was comforting for Janerose that she had found a stable environment for her children.

It was in this town that she eventually met an Austrian expertise Wolfgang who was responsible for water and hygiene in the organization that had sent him. As she served a group of foreigners, her beauty overtook this one man. Her beauty and over politeness overwhelmed Wolfgang. He had been to Uganda several times before but he had never been interested in the women there but this particular girl caught his eyes.

There was something fragile about her, a kind of sorrow that reached out to those around her though unarticulated. She seemed to be a puzzle in her simple ways. These facts awoke his instincts. He wanted to know her better. As he left the restaurant he gave her a big tip.

'Why do I deserve this big tip?' she questioned herself.

Janerose looked at the money in her hand and did not know how to deal with the situation. So she went into the kitchen and handed the money to the cook.

'A customer gave me this money after paying his bill,' she said

Then the cook said. 'That's your tip unless you want to give it to me. Keep it, you need it more than me'. This sum was bigger than her little salary, it would buy a bed for her children before she moved out. That day Janerose walked home delighted. As she slept that night she prayed for the stranger who had given her the money. She had never experienced kindness before, all what she knew was ruthlessness.

The next three months she included the stranger in her daily prayers for God's protection. It was done out of pure joy for someone helping her without knowing who she was and indeed God answered her prayers. The stranger appeared again. This time he was not shy to show his feelings for her. He smiled at her in a special kind of manner. Janerose noticed that he was overfriendly, and tried to create conversations, sometimes these conversations did not make sense but she appreciated that he had showed kindness. So she played along. When he asked to meet her in the evening this did not come as a surprise. She had heard stories of foreigners who had married her fellow countrywomen, and they were doing well in life. So there was no pretence. She knew what to expect. After work she went home and talked to granny about the stranger and her intention to meet him. She did not want to hide anything from her because she stayed with her children as she went to work and felt obliged to disclose her movements, after all granny was very honest and had established a kind of unspoken trust. After granny had consented she left to meet her stranger at the appointed time and place.

When they met Wolfgang introduced himself officially and confessed what he felt about her.
'He is too direct!' she thought. Therefore she opened up
'I am 20 years old and have two children, and live with an elderly woman whom I met through the church'. She added, 'I am from Northern Uganda and suffered the conflicts...' then she stopped. 'Do I have to reveal about my traumatised episode now?' she thought. 'It is too much!' So she remained quiet. It was painful to recall the difficult circumstances under which she had lived. Suddenly, Janerose asked to leave. Wolfgang was puzzled. 'Have I said something to offend you?' but being an intelligent man he knew there was more that she carried within her. Quickly, he escorted her home and promised to see her when he came back from Kampala, and not to complicate his feelings he said a quick goodbye and he left.

When they met again. Janerose was jolly and asked for time to tell her history and trauma. Wolfgang was patient but he knew that whatever she had experienced he would help her, maybe organize psychotherapy for her. The revelation about her past did not stop Wolfgang from loving her. It was not long and Wolfgang declared his love openly, he wished to marry her if she had no objections. Janerose did not see the reason that could stop her from marrying and starting a new life together. Things seemed to have overtaken her. The changes in her life were happening too quickly; and deep down in her heart she knew that she could not waste time, she would grab this opportunity.

Soon she found herself in a new country, she was only 21 years old. She was over the moon. Her kids remained with the granny as she went to start a new life until she was settled down. However life would soon change for Janerose because her husband travelled a lot. She found herself bored and began to frequent pubs. It is here that she met Kiddo, and out of loneliness they drank together. Sometimes Janerose's husband would be gone for many months. This gave her the opportunity to meet Kiddo who had unstable character and unhealthy behaviour. He was a drug addict. In the beginning he concealed his addiction from her but as their relationship developed he introduced her to it. Without his daily dose he became paranoid and this led to fighting especially if he could not get money. He beat her but she thought she loved him and looked for a good life.

Janerose led a double life; that of a normal housewife and that of a drug addict. It was two years later that Wolfgang discovered what she was up to. Janerose became aggressive and uncompassionate. Therefore he thought that the only solution to change her was to bring her children over. He blamed himself for being away but the job was well paid and he could not stay around to look after her. He loved her, and arrangements were made and her children arrived.

Soon a school was found and the children began to learn the German language. This new role and responsibility was too much for Janerose who had led a carefree life. She had forgotten what it meant to be a mother. Sometimes she felt like a trapped animal. She did not take the responsibility of bringing up her children seriously. Instead she felt it was Wolfgang's duty after all he is the one who brought them over. Sometimes, she blamed her own mother and relatives. So every time she was caught guilty she put the blame on someone. In some way she neglected her children. Alcohol and drugs filled up her time. She failed to supervise their schoolwork, and did not give them advice on the challenges they experienced everyday. It was the eldest daughter Sheila who was then 8 years old that took the role of a mother to see that there was food on the table and that the house was kept clean. Before the end of the year the school was aware of what was happening, and intervened.

Many years later Sheila remembers the pain she went through as she accompanied Tanisha to do therapy.
'Mum was never there for us! Only the lawyers who fought to get us back from child custody'. Wolfgang was given the sole custody of the children. He was lucky that the company accepted to have him stationed in Vienna.

Tanisha the youngest daughter recalls a confrontation that she had with her mum those days. 'It was heart breaking to see my mother full of drugs. She was like a zombie and sometimes she did not recognise me. Today I still blame her for my difficult life because she neglected us. I never experienced love. I do not know what love is, or what it means to be loved. My mother was not there when we needed her advice about our body changes or what one feels when being attracted to the opposite sex'. She stopped and looked around at those listening to her in the therapy class.

Then she continued. 'Even when I was mistreated in school or bullied she failed to protect me. So all my life I have been a very bitter girl and have expected my mother to apologize for what she did to us. I ended up finding solace and comfort in food because of being traumatized by my mother's rejection. Whenever I felt sad and low, I ate and this made me feel better. In fact that way, I discovered that food compensated for my feeling. Today, I am almost 200kgs. Do you think I am happy when people look at me? I am frustrated!'

These outbursts shocked everyone sitting around her. It was an honest cry for help; she was attending a youth mentorship programme to support children with trauma.

Then she recounted how she had been raped in the park. Suddenly, the room went quiet. It was the youth leader who placed her hands on her shoulders.
'It was terrifying to see myself like that. The damage was enormous and I felt no activity in my body as I lay there crying for my mother to come and rescue me. It was hard and I do not want anyone to experience what I went through' she said staring on a spot on the floor. It shocked everyone that she was so brave to have recounted this episode.

'Because of fear and shame I kept it to myself. I did not want anyone to imagine that I was a bad girl and that is why it had happened to me. I crawled home and sneaked to the bathroom. I cleaned myself and then disappeared to bed and wept. My stepfather Wolfgang, God bless his soul, suspected that something terrible must have happened to me. Even his continuous persuasion did not penetrate my hardened soul to tell him about the nasty experience. I was never the same after that day. Instead I ate and ate until I felt sick. I was trying to suppress the emotions that threatened to destroy me.'

Then she paused and focused her eyes on the ceiling. She was afraid to look at anyone. 'When my mother did not come home to visit me that day, it was the last straw. She had been informed of my sudden quietness, and locking myself up in my room where I just played loud music. Maybe it was a way of dealing with my problem alone. After that I heard that my mother had come in conflict with the law for destruction of property and fighting. She could not control her impulsive and anti-social behaviour. It was not long before she began to spend her time in prison. When she was not in prison she was engaged in serious crime or drinking in the bars'.

Everyone in the room was fighting their own battles but Tanisha's battle was quite a difficult one; she had many issue to deal with.

'You need to confront your mum about these issues. Let her know what you feel otherwise you will be carrying this burden all your life,' advised the expert.

Tanisha was now 24 years old; she had turned down every boy that was interested in her. She could not open up. She was still afraid and could not trust anyone. It was important that she completed this therapy so that she could regain her confidence in humanity again.

Before doing therapy Tanisha had listened to her sister Sheila who had encouraged her to consider professional help. Sheila had studied psychology and now worked for an international organization. She had gone to work in the Southern Sudan to help traumatised girls. Now it was Sheila's turn to speak to the group about her work in Sudan. Everyone paid attention, and Tanisha was proud of her sister's work. And in a very confident voice Sheila spoke, 'these children witness unimaginable atrocities. Some of these kids are prone to bedwetting and relentless nightmares that keep them awake at night. So the children attend family support centre programs, which provide psychosocial activities and legal help. I run activities that help children to overcome their trauma when it is too complicated, and they cannot talk about their experiences. These children are allowed to draw pictures of what they witnessed as a process to help them work out their feelings. After that they can talk about it or try to find the meaning of what actually occurred.'

Then she continued. 'It is in studying psychology that I was able to overcome my own experiences with my mother. I saw my mother's difficult childhood, explosive anger and drugs as some of the reason she cannot lead a stable life. I believe that she has to make the choice to adjust and overcome the addictions if she wants to leave a normal life. She is totally responsible for the choices she made and has made. She had the opportunity to reject all these habits, and was offered a comfortable home. My stepfather provided her with everything. Even when Tanisha and I gave up on her, he did not; he still loved her and held onto her,' Sheila stopped talking.

Then she added. 'One day I remember how she came to school to pick me up. I was embarrassed. She was so drunk that she could not walk'. Everyone could feel the pain as she continued to narrate. 'Then she had these continuous fights with everyone in Africa Sunshine Den. Although I loved the taste of the food there, I refused to accompany her because she was always involved in some scene that left us devastated'. She looked at her sister who was hearing these bad experiences for the first time.

'Then one day my stepfather returned home from work to find men full in the house, all drunk and partying. He was decent enough to call the police so that peace and order could return in our lives. My mother went on to call him names and destroyed his car but he forgave her. Somehow he felt guilty that he had brought her to Austria and did not want anything to happen to her. His biggest fear was to loose her. That is why he tolerated all the difficulties. She refused to work or even attend the language classes. Today I know what he must have felt'.

Then retrospectively she went on. 'I am happy that I studied psychology and have a chance to save other people's children but now I want to take a year off to take care of my mother. She is still my mother and I love her no matter what. She is ageing and very sickly. I will assist her to confront her addiction and if necessary accompany her for rehabilitation. The time to put blames is over,' she completed. With these words everyone clapped. Yes a mighty clap that filled the hall. Sheila had overcome her negative emotions and had found a forgiving heart. Then Tanisha stood up and hugged her sister. They felt renewed to confront a new beginning.

After the therapy session Sheila decided to walk home and went through the second district. She went to Prater Entertainment Park; and then towards a small building that brought back bad memories of her mother. She mastered all her courage and stood there studying the place; the building had been a small pub that had now closed. The images of her mother stoned and screaming made her wince. The worst is when she found her naked and displaying herself for the rest of the staggering drunk crowd.

She remembered how she used to go there only when she had to look for her mother especially when she had disappeared for many days.

Till today, Sheila cannot understand why her mother loved that place. Maybe it was the comradeship in alcohol and drugs. Maybe they understood her language better. Then she remembered the day she walked into the pub as usual to look for her, only to find a big police search with big dogs.

'Everyone was lying on the floor with their hands up. I was ushered in with commands to be searched. The dogs frightened me as my toes curled up and intense fear gripped me. I found my hands shaking and could not find words to explain why I was there. The search embarrassed me. 'Where is your passport?' asked the officer. My fingers shook as I tried to reach inside my bag. The officer who was waiting for my passport had a balaclava. I could not read the expression in his eyes. After I had handed over my passport I was asked to move to the next room. The lighting was poor so I did not see the woman officer waiting at the corner for me till she asked me to undress'.

'Did I hear right?' I hesitated.

'Yes, remove all your clothes and walk over here!' came the command.

'Having to undress and to have my body searched was degrading!

'Worst still I had to lie down next to the drunkards,' she paused.

'Then in the crowd I spotted my mother who seemed to be enjoying the happenings. She teased the police and kept on asking when they would finish because she was thirsty.'

She recalled. 'My mother screamed and was excited that I had joined her to drink and entertain men. Come here my daughter let me introduce you to Karli my darling and Klaus his friend. You can pair up with Klaus after he has bought a few beers.' Sheila kept quiet.

'Sheila is a beauty and will make a good wife. What do you think Sheila?' My mother walked towards me and then fell with a thud. She was stark naked'.

Sheila was ashamed and has never forgotten that incident. It changed her life completely. She left the country in order to be very far from her mother who had become a source of humiliation and pain; but she had now come back to redeem her from this awkward life and care for her. The experiences in Southern Sudan had taught her to forgive. She had met people with worse traumas then her mother.

So standing in front of this small building was like a determination to leave her mother's past behind; it was a confrontation of the past ghosts. She saw hope and a new future for her family. As she walked away she was overwhelmed with new emotions, and a few drops of tears escaped her eyes as she felt a leap of joy. Her steps increased as she walked away and headed home to her mother where she would lay out her plan and the way forward.

Chapter 10

Fiona's first experience

There were lots of beautiful trees in the big forest surrounding their little country house near the lake in the environments of Salzburg. A small path led through the forest and ended up at a small hill. Fiona's children loved to jump into the lake and swim to the opposite side. She was scared that they would drown. She had never learned to swim and her fear was deep. Fiona had come to Austria as a young girl of nineteen years old. She had married a fifty four year old man who she had met in her country where she had worked as part of a traditional dance group. The dance group entertained tourists in the hotels and in the surrounding discos, and entertainment places.

Now settled in Austria, her journey was long. Fiona was full of dreams as she left Kenya for the first time. She remembers how she had dropped out of school to look after her two children, Marion and Ben. Oh! Fiona had become pregnant first at the age of fourteen. The school bursar had impregnated her. She was sent away from school to keep the pregnancy a secret, then she had given birth to a bouncy handsome boy. Her biggest problem was that she could not go back to school. Those days it was difficult for a girl to go back to school after giving birth. A difficult life had begun for her. She had to fend for her child with very little support from her parents. Her parents were poor, and they could not fully provide for her and the children. Just her school fee was a problem.

As she watched her children ran across the backyard with the Alps Mountains in the background she recalled how she had been forced to leave home at an early age to work on a coffee plantation. It was hard work but she needed the money. It was here that she met Mr Komet the farm foreman. In the beginning he was very nice to her, he provided for her midday lunch and often offered her a lift back home.

Fiona was very happy for those little favours. Sometimes he threw a few coins for her to buy a few provisions for her child, she found him to be really nice, kind and understanding.

She remembers her second pregnancy like it was yesterday. It happened after three months when Mr. Komet invited her to accompany him to Nairobi. He informed her that he would take the coffee reports to his boss in Nairobi, and he also wanted to present her for a new job that had been advertised in the company. So how could she reject such an enticing offer?

Like in a dream she walked into her big modern kitchen to prepare lunch for her children who were swimming in the lake. She loved them so much. They were a source of joy to her life. Then as she placed the pan on the fire, she recalled that before leaving for Nairobi Mr Komet had given her money to buy presentable clothes. Quickly, Fiona went to the nearest town in Muranga and bought a beautiful dress and also had her hair done. When she met Mr Komet he was speechless, the fifteen-year-old girl had turned into a beauty queen. He whistled and licked his lips. He enjoyed looking at her. It was mid afternoon when they left for Nairobi, and a Friday for that matter. Fiona was happy to sit in the exclusive car; it was the only car of its type in that area. She sat in front seat, it was an opportunity to observe how the car was driven, and also to enjoy the views. The trees seemed to move fast as they sped on the highway. There were big coffee, sisal and passion fruit plantations along the way. She swallowed all these views with her eyes; it was an unbelievable sight.

After the food was ready Fiona took it to the oak dining table and called for her children to come. She had cooked Wiener schnitzel that was everyone's favourite in the house. After serving them food she went upstairs to feed the dog. She then recalled what she felt as they approached Nairobi, she was overwhelmed. The neat houses, the sanitized streets, flowers and trees made her shiver. Oh! She wished she lived in this part of the country. This was the dream she had seen in her sleep, living in a posh place. What she was experiencing now was better than the pictures that she had seen in schoolbooks. This was the real heaven. She gasped as she was brought out of the reality when Mr Komet announced that they would first eat lunch at Safari Club hotel.

Fiona was very tall for her age and after the birth of her baby she had put on some weight, so she looked quite mature. The beauty of this girl did not escape those who laid their eyes on her. She was very brown that a lot of people thought that she was of a mixed race. Her long hair spread out on her shoulders and gave her an elegant look. Her very large eyes gave her that startling innocent look. Mr Komet surveyed her before they headed for the restaurant. As they walked in all heads turned. Fiona was shining; the beauty, her figure, hairstyle and walk made everyone give her a second look. Mr Komet enjoyed and soaked in all the attention they got.

They walked to a table he had reserved and pulled out a chair for her. Fiona was a quick learner, and a good learner for that matter. She was polite and well behaved; this did not escape Mr Komet's attention.

As Mr Komet made their orders she did not argue or question anything he did. Fiona ate what had been ordered. She observed him and imitated everything he did. He was happy, that she was not an embarrassment. He looked at her with a lot of satisfaction. After lunch, they drove to the city centre and then parked his car inside Lillian towers. It was a members club, only members were allowed in. The receptionist and other staff greeted Mr Komet, a man full of wealth. The picture she had of him before was of a foreman employed to manage the coffee plantation.

When the pageboy escorted Mr Komet to a double room he had booked, Fiona was mesmerized at the majestic designs she saw. Oh! The huge soft carpet! The chandeliers! and the big mirror with a golden colour! She was so struck by the beauty of the room that she forgot to ask if that was the office they were supposed to hand in the report. The room had a big dining table, cupboards, TV and Fiona rushed to the large window as she exclaimed at the beauty below, the rushing cars and people. They were on the 9th floor of the hotel. She had never been in a storied building before. Her heartbeat quickened. Is this the heaven they talk about? Her eyes were bright and she felt happy. She had never been happy like this before. She remembered their ride in the lift; still she could not understand how it worked. Anyway, for now she was happy and did not want to spoil the occasion. Then she heard the door close and the pageboy was gone, but when he returned he was carrying a tray with crystal glasses and a bottle of wine, which he placed on the coffee table. Before he left Mr Komet gave him a generous tip, it must have been a big one because the pageboy bowed and thanked him so many times.

Then Mr Komet went to the table and picked up the bottle. The only drink or alcohol Fiona knew was from the small sip of wine she took on Sundays in her Catholic church. She could not pretend that she knew how a bottle of wine looked like. Now here was one right in front of her. Next Mr Komet poured it into the glasses. Fiona did not know how to re-act she just sat there. Mr Komet handed her a glass that she quickly took. She was excited. At first it was bitter so she spit it out, she did not like the taste. The look on her face said it all but Mr Komet coaxed her.

'Drink! It will make you feel good!'
 Fiona looked at his face. She didn't like it but she was afraid to offend him.
 So she closed her eyes and took a long sip. She ignored the bitter sour taste and swallowed. The immediate reaction she felt was that she was light and floating. Then a second sip and she began to laugh. Soon her glass was empty she refilled it and then drained the glass, and soon she was talking on top of her voice as she told jokes that made Mr Komet happy.

Had he forgotten their mission to present the reports to the boss? She thought.
When they finished the bottle they found themselves dancing to the music that poured from the hidden stereo. It was

a slow dance that merged them together. Fiona did not reject Mr Komet advances. She just stood there, and allowed him to do everything he wanted. How soon had she forgotten the pregnancy but she trusted Mr. Komet to be a gentleman? She felt safe with him and did not see any danger.

She remembers how he sang the song.

'Let me love you forever! Oh yes!

You are my sweet my lover!

So honey let me love you!

Oh! Yes!

Fiona joined in the song because it was a song that sang on the radio all the time. She interjected with the Kikuyu and Swahili version that increased his happiness.

Mr Komet must have been a funny young man. Although he was old he danced to the next song.

'Honey you are my shining star

Don't you go away!'

Somehow these songs made Fiona so happy and she giggled a lot in that shy girlish behaviour that pumped up Mr Komet's blood flow.

When she finally fell asleep she was so tipsy and could not remember what had happened. The bed was so comfortable, welcoming and warm. The sigh of Mr Komet beside her did not make her afraid. She felt lucky, but how long would that luck go on?

Fiona was brought out of her flashback as she realized that the pudding she was cooking was burning. It was Ben who alerted her. She would have to make pancakes, and then prepare new pudding for the family later. She gave them the pancakes with chocolate and lay on the garden couch on her balcony. Then she closed her eyes and relaxed.

In her flashback she recalled the next morning at Lilian Towers, Mr Komet had ordered for breakfast. Fiona was flabbergasted, breakfast in bed. Oh! The surprise was too much for this village girl. They ate their breakfast in silence. Fiona realized that Mr Komet did not want to look at her in the eyes. She felt uneasy especially when he suggested that he would drive alone to the offices and pick her up on their way back to the village.

What about the job? She thought.

These thoughts were interrupted as Mr Komet told her to shower quickly and wait for him at the reception area. Fiona wondered what had gone wrong.

She did as instructed. Fiona went down alone, and sat at the reception. When Mr Komet walked into the reception, he paid the bill as someone brought his car to the front of the hotel.

He left without looking at her, but he had told the waiters to serve her the club juice. They brought her magazines and newspapers which she enjoyed reading. Four hours passed, and she was still waiting at the reception. Lunch was served at the dining hall.

An elderly man led her to a table.

'How old are you?'

This question took her by surprise she did not know what to say.

'You are my grandchild's age', the old man commented.

Somehow she was so honest that she said, 'Fifteen'

The old man shook his head.

'How do you know Mr Komet?'

'He is my foreman in the village'.

She timidly answered. He looked up at her

'You are young, beautiful, and intelligent, you should be in the company of young people like you.'

Fiona stared.

'Mr Komet always brings young girls like you here, be careful,' he finally said.

Fiona swallowed heavily. Her mouth was dry as she digested these words.

She tried to remember everything but there was a gap in time. She could not find an explanation. Fiona had been too drunk to remember if she had slept with Mr Komet but before she could ask the old waiter for more information, Mr Komet appeared.

They drove in silence all the way to Muranga. A few kilometres before their village, he dropped her at the bus stop, and then gave her some money and asked her to find her way home.

At this point a small drizzle woke her up from her recollections, and then she walked away from her balcony to prepare to go to work. Fiona had found a job as a home nurse after completing the German language classes, and nursing courses. It had taken her about five years to attain a diploma but she was grateful to her husband Kurt.

Fiona went to work, and when she came back home she made herself a cup of hot chocolate and sat on the big couch in the study room. Then she remembered that fateful Monday as she went to the factory as usual and then found a farm worker who was waiting to tell her that she had been sacked. The news came as a shock, and she was turned away at the gate. Adamantly, she refused to go and waited for Mr Komet, after all she thought that he loved her and they had a relationship. When he arrived he drove through the gate and asked the gateman not to allow her in.

Fiona stood at the gate the whole day but Mr Komet did not want to see her.

In the evening she walked back home with a heavy heart, a broken heart! She thought she was special but all of a sudden she was now alone, and she remembered her mother's words. 'Don't get pregnant again! In one year you can go back to school!'

Her dreams were shattered. A few months later she discovered that she was pregnant again. There was no one who she could share her misery with. She could not even carry out an abortion even if she wished to do so, because she had no money. Fiona was once again alone. Mr Komet had enticed and tricked her. Her efforts to contact him were fruitless. He did not want to be associated with her, and he would not risk his marriage because of a poor young girl.

Fiona would have to start again from zero. The thought of two children awoke suicidal thoughts in her but she was a coward. No, she was not going to commit suicide she would face her predicament. She decided to keep the pregnancy and give birth. She would start a new beginning somewhere; destination was unknown. Fiona touched her stomach that was like a small ball and felt a lot of love for the unformed baby. A small smile appeared on her mouth. It was a smile that was short lived. Fear overwhelmed her. She wondered how she could explain to her parents that she was pregnant again? The thought alone sent her legs trembling. She had saved very little money that would make no difference to her life, so she had to act quickly but she did not know how. She looked at the corner of the house and saw the empty water pot. Her family didn't have a water tap so she would have to go to the river that was three kilometres away to fetch water. It was a good opportunity to extend her thoughts away from her mother.

At the river Fiona sat on the stones that were near a bridge. She had a flashback of Mr Komet who had taken advantage of her. He had used her inexperience to lure her into sex. She was so trusting and did not imagine that he would discard her but he had done it. He had forgotten her beauty and slim figure so soon.

'How could he?' she thought? She tried to rewind the time she had spent in the factory. It had been a good working place but Mr Komet had interfered with her dreams. Her dreams of returning to school!

She was bitter. She felt betrayed and used.

Then Fiona was quickly brought back to reality when the herds' boy brought their cattle to drink water. They whistled and brought the cows closer to the river as they sang romantic songs. The songs were meant for Fiona but she was so troubled that she didn't recognize Njagi the soloist. He added her name to the words of the song but she did not react.

'Fiona Kacheri, the village beauty, listen to my heart that is looking for you.

See how my eyes are held captive; your smooth curves are worthy three goats, ten sheep and six cows. See the riches I have for our bride price! Fiona Kacheri marry me marry me'.

Njagi realized that Fiona had not paid attention to his song. He was not disappointed; it was an opportunity for him to approach her. He took his club and machete and swaggered towards her.

He called her, 'sweet heart honey, dream of my life, the queen of Mathioya River and future wife of Njagi'.

But there was no reaction! Not even anger or any giggling.

Njagi wondered, what had become of Fiona. A few months before Fiona would have laughed and joked with Njagi but now she wore a haggard look. The brightness in her eyes had disappeared. There was a kind of sadness that he could not explain. She turned and stared at him with no smile on her face. This look worried Njagi. They had grown up together; in fact they were neighbours who had played in this same river. Njagi and Fiona had chased butterflies together. They had played mother and father. Njagi had even made jokes of Fiona's growing breasts in her puberty phase while she had laughed at his little spiky growing beard. She had tried to pull out the spiky like hair on his face, and then she had been thrilled to see his little muscles hardening on his thin arms. The two had shared a funny childhood. They had separated when Njagi had attended Metumi primary while Fiona had gone to Tumu Tumu Girls. Usually they had met over the school holidays but it was only when Fiona got pregnant that their relationship changed.

Njagi had been disappointed but he did not allow the pregnancy to interfere with the brotherly love they had for each other. Njagi had visited Fiona during her pregnancy, he had grown to love the little boy when he was born and had often brought little things, and somehow he had decided to forgive

Fiona during her pregnancy. He had never betrayed his love for her; he had hampered the secret to make her his wife. He would bring up the boy as his own but Fiona was all the while unaware of Njagi's intention.

Today there was a kind of silence that scared Njagi. He felt that she had become too cold but he would not pester her. Once the cows had drunk enough he herded them towards south and said goodbye to the silent Fiona. Fiona just gazed at the clear running water. It brought back memories of her grandmother who had loved and supported her. She was the most wonderful and patient person she knew. They had often shared secrets and little jokes about her father and uncles who spent most of the time enjoying the local brew. Fiona's grandmother loathed lazy men. Her advice to Fiona was to find a hardworking man who would look after her but now she was gone. She had died when Fiona was in school. She missed her especially now that she needed someone to talk to. As she sat there she did not realize that so much time had passed. Oh! Her mother would be angry. So she quickly filled her can and tied it with a leather rope, and the hanging part of the rope she placed it on her head and then she stood up. This was an art she had practiced so many times. She had perfected it. She did not require a second person to assist her to lift it.

On the way she made quick steps because she still had to fill the big water tank. It required her to make several trips to the river. Today she felt different a bit tired and when she got back home the following words startled her.
'I knew it! I knew it! You cannot put your legs together. I warned you but you did not listen, see what you have done'.

Fiona was shocked. She looked down. Fear filled her. It was the reality she had been trying to avoid. How would she explain to her mother? She was speechless. At that moment, she had no answer. Silently she walked into the house and went into the kitchen. The fire had died off. She quickly rekindled it and fed it with dry firewood.

When her mother walked in the kitchen she felt trapped. She prayed that her mother would not bring up the subject again. As if her mother had read her thoughts, she asked her to sit down on the small wooden stool next to the big water pot that cooled their drinking water. Little sweat formed on her forehead, her breathing increased and she waited to be banished from home. The words that came out of her mother's mouth were so soothing that she began to cry. They were not tears of relief but tears of a mother's understanding. She wept openly and like a rising volcano she opened her heart to her mother. Words poured out of her mouth, the speed at which she spoke left her mother confused.

'Slow down! Please take your time', her mother said.

Fiona retold her story to the time she began working at the factory and how she had met Mr Komet who had pretended to be a gentle man but he had misused her trust.

'Why did you not talk to me about his plans for the trip to Nairobi?' questioned her mother.

'I thought he was a kind hearted person who was interested in me'. Fiona meekly answered.

'I should not have allowed you to leave home,' regretted Fiona's mother.

'But it was important that you get a job that would help you build your future and that of your son.'

'I'm sorry ma, I know I have disappointed you'.

It was not my intention to bear a second child without getting married.

Fiona looked at the wall.

'As for now I am ashamed as a mother! The villagers will look down upon me. A daughter with two children out of wedlock! Oh! What did I do wrong? My hopes were set in you to deliver this family from poverty. As a little girl you did well in school and my dreams were to see you educated, get a good job, and probably build for me a house like that one of Mr Njoroge'.

A sharp pain went through her heart. Her mother's words were too depressing but she promised herself to find a way out of her misery. She had heard from Nyawira that in Mombasa she could find work with the tourist hotels even with little education. Fiona swore in her heart that she would give birth and then convince her mother to look after the baby as she worked to finance them. These thoughts brought a short-lived smile. She would talk to Nyawira who would connect her to her cousins in Mombasa.

That day Fiona was tired and retired early to bed. She sought solace in her little son and held him tight as she slept. The next morning her mother accompanied her to the nearest clinic where she went for a pregnancy test check up, somehow her mother had accepted her daughter's predicament, and would support her. She would not allow anyone to ridicule her. As they walked home, her mother made a few jokes.

'You know your beauty is your downfall but maybe one day it will be your advantage!'

Suddenly, they sang together a song normally sang for a bride. The song gave them hope for a while. It helped them relax and forget their worries; Fiona was determined to change her life, and that of her unborn baby. She had saved a little money that would enable her to buy a few things in preparation for her baby.

As the months went by her pregnancy grew, soon the whole village was talking about it. They blamed her for being a loose and cheap girl who fell for every trick. It hurt Fiona but she had no choice but to ignore the bad remarks that were said. She held her head high. This determination helped her build a wall around herself. Fiona stopped caring about what people said about her, she went to the market with her protruding stomach, attended church service on Sunday, and joined in communal work. She devised a direct eye contact strategy that stopped many mouths from uttering negative remarks. The pride she felt strengthened her weak position. It gave her energy to go about her daily routine.

Soon she gave birth to a baby girl. A pretty brown girl with long hair! Somehow she was happy that the baby did not portray any features of Mr Komet. The baby looked like her. Mmh! In short she admired her daughter, the love of a mother. All the devastating matters were forgotten. It was a reward, the joys of motherhood. Fiona felt a new hope. Hope represented in the little bundle she held in her hands.
Fiona's baby had been born at home. A village midwife had assisted her. She would be forever grateful to this kind woman who had refused to accept the little money she offered for her services. It was a human gesture that touched her heart. It was a kind blessing after the gossip and rumours

that had been spread about her and her family. That evening a group of women visited her to welcome the new member of family. They brought clothes and food for her. Songs of praise for the baby were sung. This gesture renewed Fiona's goal to begin a new chapter.

When the baby turned one year Fiona asked her mum if she could leave for Mombasa to join Nyawira's sisters.

'I'm not a store for children. Remember this is the last one that I will look after'.

'Thank you mother! I will not disappoint you.' She jumped like a little Dik Dik gazelle'. Pride filled her heart.

'Before you leave visit Rosa at the clinic I have talked to her', her mother said.

At first Fiona pretended not to understand what her mother meant but her statement was said with a kind of finality. Fiona squirmed. If she did not go her mother would be disappointed. So she went to the clinic. Rosa was waiting for her.

'Yes, your mum talked to me. She is worried about you, you may get pregnant again yet you do not have a job.'

Fiona felt embarrassed that they had discussed about her private life, sexuality a topic that was taboo in her culture.

Rosa continued. 'You need to do family planning'. Fiona cringed

Suddenly, Rosa stared at her, and then pulled out several strange things. One item looked like a small snake, the other like a small cup but it was the pill that Fiona concentrated on, and she listened carefully to the explanations and instructions. Afterwards Rosa concluded.

'I would advice you to take the coil because you may forget to take your pill'.

Rosa did not wait for Fiona's answer or choice of the best family planning method. She asked her to go to the next room and get herself ready.

The coil was installed and she was free to leave.

Four weeks later, Fiona boarded Malindi bus and headed for Mombasa. In her wooden box she had a few presentable dresses and a few other things that she owned. She had no handbag, and had tied her little money in a handkerchief that she had tucked away in her bra. Frequently, she kept on touching her bra to make sure that the money was still there. When they reached Mtito Andei everyone alighted the bus. Those who had money spend on Fanta, meat pies or samosa. Fiona ate some bananas her mother had given her and drunk some millet porridge she had carried in a bottle.

It was not long before they reached Mombasa, Nyawira's sister Monica was waiting for her. As she alighted from the bus she did not recognize her. Her skin colour had changed. Monica looked like a white girl; she had bleached her skin and added extensions on her hair. The shoes she wore glittered in the sun, and a pair of wide brimmed sunglasses covered her face. This appearance reminded her of a Hollywood actress. Fiona stood there till a warm hand touched her shoulders. It was the laughter and joy that made her recognize Monica. They hugged each other for a long time. Then they walked towards the bus stop where they took a colourful mini bus and went to Tudor. Monica lived in Tudor; she had married a tour guide Mr Mutiso who organized safaris and entertainment for tourist from Sweden, Germany, Italy and Switzerland. Fiona was astounded. She had never seen such beautiful houses, and especially the location next to the Indian

Ocean. The humidity made her sweat profusely but that did not bother her. It was joy that overwhelmed her. A new hope was on the horizon. She felt deep in her heart that she would succeed and she did.

Mr Mutiso connected her to the hotel manager of Two Fishes Hotel. There were no jobs available in the hotel but she could join the hotel traditional dancers to earn some money till a position was found at the reception or in the kitchen. It was important for her to start somewhere. The first day she practiced dancing and singing. Fiona was a quick learner; it was not difficult to keep up with the professionals. She was young and energetic. As she danced she thought of her two children in the village and prayed to work hard. 'If I can earn enough money, maybe I could bring them to live with me,' she thought. It all depended on her work.

That evening she received her first pay it was not much. In her determination she would save every single coin so that she could rent a room near the hotels. The distance to Monica's house was consuming all her earnings. It was not long before she found someone she could share a room with. It was a good idea, and after six months of working, Fiona finally fetched her children from the village.
It was a happy reunion, she found a small girl who could assist with looking after the children, and life was fair to her.

As the year came to an end, a young white man, a visitor in the hotel became interested in Fiona. In the beginning she was irritated. The looks from her co-dancers made her embarrassed. She was afraid that they would say ugly things behind her back. She had heard about many horrific stories told about white people. The thought alone of going out with one was enough to make her recoil but the white boy did not stop pursuing her. Her beauty, long neck and big oval eyes fascinated him. It became his routine to watch the three entertainment performances every evening, and his eyes did not leave Fiona's face. Every time they ended the dance performance he could be heard applauding and trying some Swahili words like (mzuri sana) meaning very well. The pronunciation of the words brought laughter and tears to most of the dancers. 'He cannot even pronounce basic words.' I thought he was educated.

Someone else commented 'but Swahili is a foreign language so it is only natural that his pronunciation sounds strange.'

One evening, Fiona stood under the palm trees close to the beach and stared at the clear sky, the number of stars fascinated her. Her fascination for the stars had begun as a little child. It was her way of relaxing and getting inner peace and strength, and sometimes it helped her forget her problems. This particular evening she was so concentrated that she did not see the white man walk up to her. It was only when he touched her on the shoulder that she turned and saw his deep blue eyes that seemed to dance as they looked at her. This was the closest that she had ever stood next to a white person. Fiona gazed. Her heart raced and she was short of words. Had her tongue disappeared?

'Hello! he said

'Mmh...Mmhh...! She stammered,

'What's your name? he asked.

'Fiona! came a small shy voice. Her voice seemed not real.

'My name is Kurt Wilhelm,' came a booming reply.

They stood there staring, gazing and seizing each other up.

Kurt was a gentleman. He extended his hand and also bowed. This surprise made Fiona laugh. In her life she had never dreamt of anyone showing her kindness. She smiled and greeted Kurt who grinned.

He invited her for a drink in the restaurant, but she was afraid of the bar manager and waiters, she preferred to have her drink outside the hotel. It could affect her job, which she desperately needed to support her two children.

A few days later Kurt asked to meet her children.

'I m sorry, I am not sure if my children and neighbours will find the idea nice.' Fiona informed him.

'That's not true Fiona,' disagreed Kurt. 'There are so many white people at the coast; it is not strange if I visit you.' Kurt insisted.

'Look at me Fiona, trust me, I do not intend to spoil your life. I was amazed at the way I saw you dancing. You are not just a beautiful girl but you have something special in you. You are intelligent, captivating and kind. I don't know you well but you have a spell on me? Kurt pleaded.

'Give me a fair chance to visit you and your children,' he went on.

Fiona was overwhelmed; these words touched her heart that had turned cold for a very long time.

'Would this be another disappointment?' she questioned herself.

She thought for a while, and then thought she had nothing to lose. Her reputation had already been ruined by her earlier relationships.

Suddenly, the ring of the bell in her house in Salzburg disturbed Fiona's reverie and she quickly jumped up from the comfortable chair to open the door. It was her mother in-law who had brought fruits and cakes for her children. The two women hugged and then admired each other's attire. As they walked into the house they exchanged pleasantries. Next Fiona made coffee for the elderly woman who had accepted her as her daughter in-law; she loved Fiona and her children. The children preoccupied her, and made her life gain meaning because she lived alone after her husband had died many years ago. The two women cooked dinner together before her mother in-law left.

As Fiona waited for her family to come home, she remembered how Kurt had pleaded with her to visit her children in Mombasa. 'Okay you can visit, but there are no buses to my area. You may have to take a taxi, which is very expensive. Otherwise you will have to trek three kilometres,' she looked at him.

Kurt asked for her address, Fiona laughed. ' I do not have a house address or number. I can only explain how to get there. You need to look for the following landmark. When you get to Likoni Ferry, take a Matatu to Fontanella, and then to Maringo. At Maringo junction you will see a big tree, and people repairing bicycles. Keep on going till you reach a small river. There is no bridge so you have to walk about five hundred meters to the chicken farm. Opposite the chicken farm is a yellow coloured building, made of palm leaves. Knock on the door and ask for my house'.

Kurt did not betray his astonishment. These directions were too much for him. How would he remember all this information?

'Do you have a phone where I can reach you if I get lost?'

'The nearest phone is in a primary school, about a kilometre away. Maybe I can wait at the primary school at twelve o'clock.'

'Oh that is a good idea. Then I will drive to the primary school and we can walk to your house together'. Kurt was very excited.

The next day Fiona woke up very early and did thorough cleaning of her humble abode. Then she scrubbed her children with such vigour that they fled from pain. Finally, she inspected her work and she was satisfied. Next, she put on her Sunday best and marched to the school, her sandals raised a lot of dust and made her feet dirty but she did not stop to clean them. At the school she explained to the clerk about the expected call. The call did not come, instead a white car appeared at the school gate. As Fiona stood to inspect the car, she saw Kurt and then dashed to join him before a lot of questions were asked. He was happy to see her.

Quickly she got into the car and they drove away as the clerk appeared at the gate. The clerk stood there flabbergasted, he did not understand the relationship between the expected call and the car. Not long, they arrived at Fiona's one roomed house where her children sat on little stools waiting patiently for the guest. Kurt was excited to see them. He shook each child's hand vigorously while patting their heads but the two children were amazed, being touched by a white man. Fiona watched this spectacular scene with a smile. Kurt did not seem to fear anything instead he showed a lot of love that they had never received from any other man.

Fiona did not own a chair and asked Kurt to sit on her bed

as she brought out food that she had cooked in the morning. She sent the bigger boy to buy soda from the kiosk behind the house. Meanwhile she served the meal. It was spiced and it brought tears to Kurt's eyes. He did not want to appear as impolite. He coughed and coughed. Suddenly, he felt sick and wanted to throw up.

'I don't like spicy food, but this one is very good.'

The children laughed, 'how could this one be very good when he was sweating and coughing?

'Even if you are hungry, you don't have to eat it. I will give you only potatoes'. Intervened Fiona.

Kurt shook his head, 'I like the spinach and the tomatoes, and you know people in Austria eat less spicy food.'

'But you are sweating!' insisted Fiona.

'The weather in Africa is hotter than in Europe'; he talked with his mouth open.

Everyone in the house knew that the sweat was because of the spicy food not the weather.

'Here is sour milk, it will cool your tongue,' Fiona commented.

Anyway from the episode the children gave Kurt a new name, 'baba moto' (hot father). As they said goodbye to him he promised to visit them in August, as he would be leaving Kenya the next day. He promised to keep in touch; he would call Fiona once a week at the primary school. Kurt wanted Fiona to stop working at the hotel. He would send her money every month to take care of her children and to pay for rent meanwhile. It was important that Fiona enrol in a course to learn computer skills and to drive a car. This information was too much for her.

How can a stranger offer to help her was this true or was it a dream?

To add on, he asked her to open a bank account where he could send her money. Fiona could not contain herself and broke down. She wept tears of joy and confusion. Since her children did not understand why their mother was crying, they too joined her and cried. They cling onto her legs. Kurt captured this moving scene in his memory. He was so touched that he too cried. As they escorted him to catch his taxi he held all their hands together and for the first time and he kissed Fiona. There was no time for the children to question this sudden behaviour. Kurt got in his car and drove away as the children continued to wave.

When they walked back home that evening there was a kind of peace Fiona had not known. She felt relaxed as she opened her door. On the table there was a white envelope, which Kurt had secretly left behind. It was addressed to Fiona. On opening it, a banker's cheque fell out. She thought it was a piece of paper, but when she looked at it she could not believe her eyes. It bore 53 but she did not understand the other figures because the words were German, 'Deutsche mark'. That night she did not sleep. How could she thank Kurt? He would be leaving early in the morning.

So she decided quickly to go to the airport to surprise him. There were no vehicles in her area that early morning. The only person who could assist her was the primary school watchman who would escort her up to the main road. She would use all her savings to hire a taxi to take her to the airport.

The next morning Fiona went to the airport as she had

planned the previous morning. When she appeared Kurt could hardly believe his eyes. It was like a fairy tale, the prince and his princess that is how he felt. It was a wonderful moment. There were still two hours left before departure. They walked into the airport coffee house hand in hand. They had no words but searched each other faces. Fiona was not ashamed to acknowledge her feelings for Kurt. She was about to speak but Kurt placed his fingers on her lips not to spoil the magical moment. He continued looking at her with a lot of awe. Finally he kissed her. Fiona was not embarrassed instead she closed the world outside and basked in Kurt's love. The coffee they had ordered turned cold. It was the waiter who alerted them when he brought the bill. Kurt paid the bill and they walked through his departure gate where they stood holding each other. They were so engrossed that they did not hear the final call for boarding the flight. Kurt was lucky that the airport was not full that morning. It was the ground hostess who saw him. She alerted him about the flight that would leave without him, so he quickly said good-bye to his love and left.

Fiona stood there, fixed to the ground as she watched the plane take off. As the plane disappeared into the blue sky, Fiona walked outside into the hot sun that dazzled her eyes. She was in a dream and was not ready to release the dream. For sometime her mind was focused on what had happened in the last week. It is only when a man asked her to make way so that he could push his luggage that she discovered that she did not know how she would get back home because she had spent all her money on the taxi. Then she remembered the cheque in her handbag. Immediately, she begged a taxi driver to take her to the nearest bank where she cashed it, and then paid the driver.

Fiona was scared to carry the money.

The sum was too much, suddenly she walked back into the bank and opened an account where she deposited almost all the money, and then took a bus to Mwembe Tayari where she bought beautiful clothes for her children and lots of food. This day she would spoil herself. She went to Hard Rock Café, a place she had never been to. She ordered a hearty meal and enjoyed it with a glass of passion juice. She felt like the actress Julia Roberts shopping on the Boulevard.

Finally, she went to the only computer college and enrolled. Fiona could begin her classes in two weeks time. After that she went home to her children. Before the end of the week she received a letter from Kurt informing her when he would call. When he called it was pure excitement. She enjoyed the moment and soon these phone calls became regular and were also a source of information from the outside world. Kurt kept his promise; he sent money regularly for her children and her course.

At the end of seven months Kurt arrived as promised. He was happy to find that Fiona had completed her diploma in computer skills, and had already begun driving lessons. Kurt stayed with Fiona in a bigger house that he rented for her. It was a happy reunion that they got to know each other better but he had only a month's holiday. It was enough for him to make a decision to invite Fiona and her children to spend Christmas with him in Austria. Then before he left he accompanied Fiona to acquire traveling documents.

At the end of his holiday Kurt visited Fiona's parents in the village in Muranga. He insisted on being open, and getting to know her relatives, which was a good sign for Fiona that Kurt had good intentions. On his departure he left a tearful Fiona who clung to him like a broken child. She had never known kindness and love. It was his loving nature that she would miss till she visited him. Kurt wished he could stay longer but he had to work. Before Christmas Kurt sent Fiona tickets and documents to enable them to travel, they had to apply for travel visa from the Austrian embassy in Nairobi. Fiona was overwhelmed by the visa requirements and the journey to Nairobi with her children. She was brave enough to make several journeys to Nairobi before they finally left for Austria. All her relatives went to the airport to see her off. It was the first time that she had visited Jomo Kenyatta international airport; it was busier than Mombasa international airport. Everyone admired her; even those who had ill-treated her, and spoken badly about her. They were all hugging her like a beauty queen. They all praised her, exaggerated their kindness and called her children future kings and queens before heading for the checking counter where they would deposit their luggage. Some of her relatives shed tears. Her biggest surprise was Nyawira her best friend who had come to say goodbye. She was happy for her friend and the new life that she would be beginning.

Eventually Fiona and her children disappeared behind the departure gate amidst ululations, cries and loud shouts of joy. A new life had begun for her as she boarded Lufthansa airlines. As she stepped into the plane she experienced a thrilling and floating effect. It was so magical, immense and comforting. She was not scared. Her concern was engulfed on how her children would react at the take off. A kind flight attendant showed them their seats and also inquired if they needed help. She helped them to buckle up their seat belts and showed them how to operate the lights and the air condition controls above their sits.

When the plane took off and picked up speed Fiona's brevity disappeared and fear increased as the plane lifted up. She felt her stomach rise and then sink, she watched her children who seemed to master fear, and did not betray any feelings that they were experiencing any changes. Fiona held herself onto her seat with so much energy that her fingers pained. Then she tried to brake the plane with her feet as it turned into its course. It is only when dinner was served that she relaxed a bit. Someone had advised her to drink a glass of wine to help her relax her nerves but she was afraid that she might fall asleep and neglect her children. The food was strange but her children savoured it and asked if they could eat her portion that she had left untouched. They ate the little cakes and asked if they could get more. This was a good sign that they had mastered the situation. At some point they fell asleep. They must have slept long because when they looked through the tiny windows they saw large white bright clouds below them.

Fiona's fear returned when they experienced turbulences but this was short lived. A short announcement came from the pilot that in about thirty minutes they would be landing at Vienna international airport. As the plane landed, Fiona was very relieved and happy to have survived her first flight ordeal. She decided to follow what other passengers were doing. She picked up her luggage and went through immigration and out to the arrival section. Her heart skipped a bit.

'Where was Kurt? He had promised to wait for them. There

were so many white people more than she had ever seen in her life.

How could she identify him in this mass of people?

She pushed her luggage as she tried to scan the area. Her fear returned.

Had he abandoned them? What would she do?

As she reached the end of the enclosed area, tears began to fill her eyes. She stopped to comfort her children who were shivering with cold. Kurt had not informed them of the cold weather so she had not dressed her children warm. She would have to keep them warm. Immediately, she opened her suitcase and asked each child to put on layers of clothes, to wear another pair of socks and to cover their heads with the Maasai clothes that she had bought as presents. Just as she had completed dressing them Kurt appeared carrying winter coats for them. He apologized for the delay because he had forgotten the coats, gloves and hats in the car, which he had parked outside. It would have been very cold for them without coats. Quickly, he helped them dress and then hugged them. It must have been dramatic for the people who watched them as Kurt led them away to the car.

The sky was grey; there was no sunshine it was foggy and very cold. Unbelievable! The coldest air Fiona had experienced in her life was from the deep freezer.

Her thoughts raced, 'how do people live in this cold? '

'Do they not get sick when they breathe cold air?' she quietly wondered.

At this thought Fiona covered her children's noses and faces. She only left enough room for their eyes. Kurt was mesmerized. He laughed so much that his eyes watered.

'Baba moto', echoed the children.

'Why was he crying?' the children wondered. His face had turned red. Kurt looked at the freezing bunch with trembling hands, and clattering teeth, and the little water drops that escaped their eyes. He regretted having parked the car far away.

To keep them away from the cold, he brought them back to the entrance and asked them to wait inside as he went for the car. Ben the big boy had a fresh haircut, which made him feel the cold more, and he shivered.

Soon he requested to put on a second pair of trousers.

'Mum, I feel like someone is cutting my legs, I cannot feel my feet.' He cried with pain. It was a heart-breaking cry. Fiona could not do anything. She stood there and watched her son suffer from cold.

'Mum, we should go back home. Kenya is warm. I do not like it here!'

He sniffled and looked at his sister Marion who was not any better but she pretended to be brave. Her trembling body betrayed how she felt. When Kurt arrived they refused to walk outside. It took sometimes to convince them that the car was heated.

'How can a car be heated?' they asked in unison.

'The cars in our country have heating systems installed to keep the car warm'.

They stared. Ben opened his mouth! Suddenly he was interested he would like to see this car that was heated. He held Kurt's hands and asked him to show him the car. Fiona and Marion followed. The car was outside near the entrance. They quickly scrambled inside and cuddled together. Kurt

assisted them to secure their safety belts and they drove away.
'Where did the tree leaves go to?
Kurt explained about the seasons of the year. In autumn the weather changes, it gets cold and the sun disappears so the trees begin to shade their leaves. Then, in winter the snow-falls and its extremely cold. The children did not understand what he talked about winter.
'What is snow?' Marion asked.
Kurt kept quiet for some time trying to find out how he could simply explain snow to the children
Ben shook his head because he could not imagine.
Soon they reached St. Polten and then drove to Linz where they stopped at the petrol station. Kurt bought them hot cho-colate and some sandwiches. They were excited to taste their first food in Austria. The joy with which they enjoyed the meal made Kurt very happy. The children did not seem to be complicated but he would regret this thought later on.

After four hours they arrived in Salzburg the second largest city in Austria. The view of the large mountains that were covered in snow awoke the children's fantasy.
In unison they questioned why the mountains were cover-ed in snow and why the water in the river was not flowing. Before Kurt could answer these questions the next question seemed to fly past his head.
'Oh look at the road! Looks like the white sand in Mombasa; and these one here are shining!' They commented as they walked.
They didn't seem to be in a hurry to run into the house. The kids were busy inspecting the environment. They were cu-rious.

'See the huge trees and the little birdhouses!' Ben exclaimed. Just before they could walk into the house, a big dog came running, and the children ran behind Kurt and hid there; but the big friendly dog jumped on Ben and he screamed, he was too afraid of dogs.

Kurt had not mentioned that he had a dog. Fiona retraced to the car. She opened the front door and jumped in. Kurt pulled the dog and comforted the children. He accompanied the dog back to the house and locked it into the visitors' room upstairs. The surprise was not yet over. As the children entered the house, three big cats appeared. Marion was shocked and jumped on the sofa.

During this time Kurt had gone back to bring Fiona! As they came back, Ben was on top of the table staring at the cats. Kurt was overwhelmed.

He did not expect this strong reaction of fear.

He murmured something like the cats and his dog are friendly; they are harmless.

This did not convince the children to come down. Soon he realized that their fear was real. He would have to find a solution for the four weeks that Fiona and the children would be around. Luckily, his mother lived three houses away, so she picked up the dog and the cats and would keep them till the children had adjusted. Fiona wanted to have a clear understanding about the animals if they decided to settle in Austria.

Soon the episode with the animals was forgotten. The kids were tired and before they retired to bed they ate the food Kurt had prepared for them but they complained about the smell of cheese, which they did not like. They refused to eat the mushroom soup because it had a funny colour. The vegetable salad was left untouched. The strong taste of vinegar was not welcome let alone the thought of eating raw vegetables. They had not seen yellow paprika, lettuce, and cucumbers. All these things were strange to them and anything unfamiliar was immediately ignored or rejected but they loved the yoghurt flavours and the sweet vanilla chocolate cake.

After that Kurt prepared a warm bath. It was an exciting, small swimming activity. As soon as they felt the warmth of the warm water, they fell asleep immediately. After a while Fiona checked on them and found that they were deep asleep. 'Wake up! You have to go to bed', she cautiously whispered. 'Take the towel and wipe your bodies dry'.
They stared at her dreamily. Marion lifted her hands expecting Fiona to help her out.
'Hold on the side of the bathtub and then step out,' she commanded.
'You will make me wet be careful!' She called out on Ben as he tried to touch her.
The two tired kids stood there unable to do what their mum commanded.

Fiona quickly helped to wipe them dry and then led them to the top floor where Kurt had recently repaired two bedrooms, without wasting time; she tucked them in bed and made her way downstairs where Kurt was waiting. They shared a glass of red wine. The taste of wine was strong, it tasted bitter and Fiona did not like it and preferred to have a beer. Soon she was asleep on the sofa. The flight, preparation, acquiring documents, visa and going to the village to bid her people farewell had been too tedious.

'Oh she is snoring!' Kurt was amazed. He took a duvet and covered her. It was reasonable to let her sleep on the sofa, Kurt put off the lights and went upstairs, and before going into his bedroom he checked on the kids. They were deep asleep but he left the doors open in case of anything.

The next day the children slept longer than usual. Kurt was up early and prepared a hearty breakfast. Fiona who was sleeping next to the kitchen did not hear the loud sounds of banging pots that came from the kitchen. When she opened her eyes it was still dark. Then she looked at the wall clock, it was 9 o'clock.

'Why is it still dark? It is 9 o'clock?

Kurt explained to her, 'in winter the nights are longer than the day and at four o'clock darkness sets in'.

Still Fiona did not understand these phenomena about time, light and darkness. In Kenya the sun rose quite early, so where was the sun? She looked through the window and saw greyness as it had snowed. Everywhere was white. The trees were covered with snow so was Kurt's car.

As she joined Kurt in the kitchen, she was full of questions.

'How can people live without the sun?'

'Where does the snow come from?'

Her questions poured like a waterfall.

How would Kurt explain all these questions?

He promised to answer all her questions when the children came down for breakfast, otherwise he would have to repeat. Fiona went in search of the children upstairs, when she entered the room Ben seemed to have disappeared under the feather cover. Then she looked down at him and felt guilty to wake him up. They had not rested well for about a week. No, she would not wake him up, she thought.

'He needs the sleep'.

Then she walked into Marion's room.

'Where was the girl? She could only see the pillow but when she touched the bed, she found her curved at the bottom of the bed and lay hidden under the big covers. The bed seemed to have swallowed her. Fiona made sure that she was alive and breathing, and then walked back to the kitchen.

'The children need to sleep and can have their breakfast later'.

Fiona and Kurt ate their breakfast. The big sausage was a puzzle. She knew the small sausages in Kenya. Kurt cut a few slices and placed them on a plate. Then he cut the next different sausage and then the next. Fiona cannot remember the number. Every time he opened the fridge he brought out different things; cold fish, bottled paprika, cucumber, onions, garlic, apricots and oranges.

This was a big surprise.

'Why do people eat cold food? She only knew hot food. On the table, everything was cold. She did not want to seem unfriendly. So she tried a few things from the cold plate. The cold slices of meat were not bad after all but the butter was cold and hard. In Kenya butter was soft and it could easily be spread on the bread. So she gave up on the butter and instead used jam.

'But don't the people feel cold after eating cold food?' She thought but did not ask the question.

These are stories she would tell her mother when she went back home. Now making the tea was the next surprise. Kurt just boiled hot water and put it in a cup, then put a tea bag in it, and then added cold milk in a small cup and brought it to Fiona.

She laughed! Surely this cannot be called tea, cold milk, ha ha ha… Tea has to boil on the fire with all the ingredients. For the first time she was not afraid to ask Kurt to allow her to cook tea the way she knew it, and had grown doing it.

Of course he smiled it was not a challenge but a request. So he led her to the cooker and explained how to use it. Although Fiona had never used an electrical cooker she was a quick learner and soon she cooked tea for everybody. As she sipped the hot tea she felt at home. The tea was too hot for Kurt who added a few cubes of ice to reduce the temperature. It was evening when the children appeared. They were happy the bed was very soft and big. They blamed their long sleep on the good bed but their mum knew that they had been very tired. Anyway she warmed the tea, and offered them what Kurt had prepared but then they chose to eat bread and jam. Fiona explained to Kurt that he would have to be patient; everything was new for them. They would need time to get used to the new food. That day they stayed indoors. It was only Kurt who went outside to free his car from snow. The fascination with snow was great.

'Do people die when they breathe in snow?' asked Marion.

Now the debate was open for all of them.

'Does your dog have special shoes to walk on the snow?' inquired Ben

Before he could answer came the next one. 'Is this snow going to stay here, won't the trees and everything else disappear?' continued Ben.

Kurt spent the evening talking and explaining about snow and the different seasons. He promised to take them out to the mountains where there was even more snow.

Fiona offered to cook rice, potatoes and meat for the children; food that was familiar to them because they had eaten very little for breakfast. After eating the meal they watched TV but the language was funny. They did not understand the language so Kurt had the task of translating. He was so tired when he went to bed.

The next day he took them out to the mountains but the children refused to get out of the car; they were afraid. They preferred to watch Fiona and Kurt build a snowman. For Fiona it was too cold that her fingers froze and became very painful but she pretended to be fine. She was setting the example for her children so as to encourage them to experience the snow. After a while the children climbed out of the car very cautiously. As they touched their first snow ever they were thrilled. No one knew what they were expecting but they did not let the magical moment go unnoticed. So they made snowballs and threw them at the figures that were bent over the snowman.

Kurt was happy that the children enjoyed their first snow experience in Austria.
Soon it was Christmas. The preparations began. A Christmas tree was decorated and everyone went shopping for presents. Kurt gave the children an allowance to buy presents. After wrapping them they placed them under the tree. This was a new experience for them. The fact that Christmas dinner was eaten on 24th evening was a bit shocking but they enjoyed the hot food, cakes and getting presents.
'Mum shall we stay here?' asked Marion.
Then Fiona replied, 'no we have to go back to Kenya after New Year'.

Kurt was amazed that the children liked the cold country. He was quick to say,

'If your mum likes it here then we can arrange'.

'Mum, Mum, please say something'.

Fiona just stared and said she would discuss it with Kurt.

Soon it was New Year 's Eve, the excitement filled the air as they went out at midnight for fireworks. Ben could not contain the adventurous spirit. He ran around like a cheetah. Kurt warned the kids about the dangers of fireworks; he did not want an accident, so his priority was to see that everything went on smoothly as they prepared for fireworks.

At midnight they could see fireworks all over the city of Salzburg. When they finished watching they went back to the house. It was difficult for the children to sleep immediately but at around three they went to bed smiling.

Two days later they were on their way back to Kenya. Kurt promised to visit them in April so that he would have completed the arrangements for the wedding. They would marry in her village and around August they would join him in Austria in time for the children to join school.

After the wedding Fiona and her children moved to Salzburg.